SOUNDS OF LANGUAGE

readers

SOUNDS OF A DISTANT DRUM

BY BILL MARTIN, JR.

Holt, Rinehart and Winston, Inc., New York/Toronto/London/Sydney

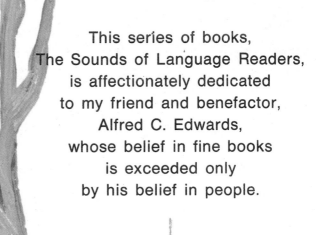

This series of books,
The Sounds of Language Readers,
is affectionately dedicated
to my friend and benefactor,
Alfred C. Edwards,
whose belief in fine books
is exceeded only
by his belief in people.

03-060735-3

Copyright © 1967 by Holt, Rinehart and Winston, Inc.
Printed in the United States of America
4607354

Acknowledgments

The Author and Holt, Rinehart and Winston, Inc., thank the following authors, publishers, agents and parties whose help and permissions to reprint materials have made this book possible. If any errors in acknowledgments have occurred, the errors were inadvertent and will be corrected in subsequent editions as they are realized.

Abingdon Press, for "How Baseball Began in Brooklyn," from *How Baseball Began in Brooklyn,* by LeGrand. Copyright © 1958 by LeGrand Henderson. Used by permission.

Allied Chemical Corporation, for the use of their photograph which accompanies the poem "Snow-bound" by John Greenleaf Whittier.

Atheneum Publishers, for "A Cliché," from *It Doesn't Always Have to Rhyme,* by Eve Merriam. Copyright © 1964 by Eve Merriam. Reprinted by permission of the publishers.

Atheneum Publishers, for "Leavetaking" and "One, Two, Three—Gough!" from *It Doesn't Always Have to Rhyme,* by Eve Merriam. Copyright © 1964 by Eve Merriam. All rights reserved. Reprinted by permission.

Basil Blackwell & Mott, Ltd., for "Last Song" by James Guthrie. Reprinted by permission.

Bodley Head Ltd., for "The Princess and the Vagabone," from *The Way of the Storyteller,* by Ruth Sawyer. Copyright 1942 by Ruth Sawyer. Reprinted by permission.

Michael Brent Publications, Inc., Port Chester, New York, for "Our Country 'Tis of Thee," excerpts from the historical cantata, *Our Country 'Tis of Thee,* narration written by Ruth Roberts, all songs written by Ruth Roberts and William Katz except the three songs, "Our Country 'Tis of Thee," "The Whole Wide World Is My Home Town," and "Opus 1920," by Ruth Roberts. The entire cantata © 1966 and 1967 by Michael Brent Publications, Inc., through which source the entire cantata is available. All rights reserved.

Carol Ryrie Brink, for her poem, "Goody O' Grumpity," as found in *Favorite Poems Old and New,* edited by Helen Ferris, published by Doubleday & Company, Inc.

C. Edward Cerullo, for the painting on page 270, "The Donner Party," by William Reusswig, from *The Illustrator in America 1900–1960,* by Walt Reed. Published by Reinhold Publishing Corporation, New York. Photographed with his permission.

Chatto & Windus Ltd., for "Lone Dog," from *Songs to Save a Soul,* by Irene Rutherford McLeod, published by The Viking Press, Inc. Reprinted by permission.

Curtis Brown, Ltd., London, for "The Two Frogs," from *The Art of the Story-Teller,* by Marie L. Shedlock, published by Dover Publications, Inc. Copyright © 1951 by Marie L. Shedlock. Reprinted by permission.

Doubleday and Company, Inc. for "comforting thoughts," by Don Marquis, copyright 1920 by New York Tribune, Inc. from *archy does his part,* a section of *the lives and times of archy and mehitabel,* by Don Marquis. Reprinted by permission of the publishers, Doubleday & Company, Inc.

Doubleday & Company, Inc., for "What is Black?" Copyright © 1960 by The Curtis Publishing Company, from the book, *Hailstones and Halibut Bones,* by Mary O'Neill. Reprinted by permission of the publishers, Doubleday & Company, Inc.

Constance Garland Doyle and Isabel Garland Lord, Sherman Oaks, California, for "Do You Fear the Force of the Wind?" by Hamlin Garland.

The Society of Authors, London, Representative for The Literary Trustees of Walter de la Mare, for the extract from "The Ride-by-Nights" by Walter de la Mare.

The Society of Authors, London, Representative for The Literary Trustees of Walter de la Mare, for "Silver" by Walter de la Mare.

Stewart In-Fra-Red, Inc., for the picture of the sandwich on page 161. Used with their courtesy.

Triangle Publications, Inc., for the illustration on pages 140–141, by Francis Spinks/Barker Black which appeared in *SEVENTEEN®* Magazine, April 1965 issue. Copyright © 1965 by Triangle Publications, Inc., and reproduced with their permission.

The Viking Press, Inc., for "Lone Dog," from *Songs to Save a Soul,* by Irene Rutherford McLeod. All rights reserved.

The Viking Press, Inc., for "The Princess and the Vagabone," from *The Way of the Storyteller,* by Ruth Sawyer, copyright 1942 by Ruth Sawyer. Reprinted by permission of the Viking Press, Inc.

The Viking Press, Inc., for the selection of text and art, "Henry Reed, Inc.," or "Monday, July 29," from *Henry Reed, Inc.,* by Keith Robertson. Copyright © 1958 by Keith Robertson. Reprinted by permission of the publishers.

Williamson Music, Inc., New York, New York, and Williamson Music Ltd., London, England, for "A Cock-eyed Optimist," from *South Pacific.* Copyright © 1949 by Richard Rodgers and Oscar Hammerstein II. Used by permission of the publishers, Williamson Music, Inc., New York, New York, and Williamson Music Ltd., London, England.

Dixie Willson, Fairhaven, New Jersey, for permission to reprint her poem, "The Mist and All," originally published in *Child Life.*

The World's Work Ltd., London, for "What Is Black?" from *Hailstones and Halibut Bones,* by Mary O'Neill. Copyright © 1960 by The Curtis Publishing Company. Reprinted by permission.

TABLE OF CONTENTS
PART I

FIGURING OUT HOW READING WORKS

PART II

RESPONDING TO READING

LEAVETAKING

Vacation is over;
It's time to depart.
I must leave behind
(although it breaks my heart)

Tadpoles in the pond,
A can of eels,
A leaky rowboat,
Abandoned car wheels;

For I'm packing only
Necessities:
A month of sunsets
And two apple trees.

A poem by Eve Merriam,
painting by Ted Rand

PIG WISPS

There was an oyster king far in the south
who knew how to open oysters and pick out the pearls.
He grew rich, and all kinds of money came rolling in on him
because he was a great oyster opener
and knew how to pick out the pearls.
  The son of this oyster king was named Shovel Ears.
And it was hard for him to remember.
  "He knows how to open oysters, but he forgets
to pick out the pearls," said the father of Shovel Ears.
  "He is learning to remember worse and worse
and to forget better and better," said the father of Shovel Ears.
  Now in that same place far in the south
was a little girl with two braids of hair twisted down her back
and a face saying, "Here we come—where from?"
  And her mother called her Pig Wisps.
Twice a week Pig Wisps ran to the butcher shop
for a soup bone. Before starting, she crossed her fingers
and then the whole way to the butcher shop kept her fingers crossed.
  If she met any playmates and they asked her
to stop and play crosstag or jackstones
or all-around-the-mulberry-bush or the-green-grass-grew-all-around
or drop-the-handkerchief, she told them,
"My fingers are crossed,
  and I am running to the butcher shop
  for a soup bone."

A story by Carl Sandburg, pictures by David Czarin

One morning, running to the butcher shop,
she bumped into a big queer boy and bumped him flat on the sidewalk.
"Did you look where you were running?" she asked him.
"I forgot again," said Shovel Ears.
"I remember worse and worse. I forget better and better."
"Cross your fingers like this," said Pig Wisps, showing him how.
He ran to the butcher shop with her,
watching her keep her fingers crossed till the butcher gave her the soup bone.
"After I get it, then the soup bone reminds me
to go home with it," she told him.
"But until I get the soup bone, I keep my fingers crossed."
Shovel Ears went to his father
and began helping his father open oysters.
And Shovel Ears kept his fingers crossed to remind him to pick out the pearls.
He picked a hundred buckets of pearls the first day
and brought his father the longest slippery, shining rope of pearls
ever seen in that oyster country.
"How do you do it?" his father asked.
"It is the crossed fingers—like this," said Shovel Ears,
crossing his fingers like the letter X.
"This is the way to remember better and forget worse."
It was then the oyster king went and told the men
who change the alphabets just what happened.
When the men who change the alphabets
heard just what happened, they decided to put in a new letter,
the letter X, near the end of the alphabet, the sign of the crossed fingers.

On the wedding day of Pig Wisps and Shovel Ears,
the men who change the alphabets all came to the wedding,
with their fingers crossed.

Pig Wisps and Shovel Ears stood up to be married.
They crossed their fingers.
They told each other they would remember their promises.

And Pig Wisps had two ropes of pearls
twisted down her back and a sweet young face saying,
"Here we come—where from?"

A Picture for Storywriting

Photograph by Arthur Beck

The Stone

The snowflakes fell gently,
collapsing of their own weight
an instant after hitting
the boy's coat sleeves,
and he grinned.
He pulled the last knot tight,
snugging the large box
to the rear carrier
of his bicycle.

In just these few minutes
the new snowfall had hidden
the last dinginess
of last week's snow
and now piled up
like sugar icing on everything.
   Tom Gentry opened his mouth,
enjoying the faint tingle
as the falling snow
touched his tongue and melted.
One flake struck his eye,
changing itself
into a warm tear
which slid down his cheek
when he blinked,
and he laughed.

He felt wonderful
this fine December morning—
proud and happy knowing
that this year he'd be giving
his mother a Christmas gift
beyond any expectation.
He tried to imagine
how surprised
and pleased she'd look
taking the beautiful mink choker
from its gaily wrapped package,
and he let out a happy yell.

   He tugged
on the clothesline rope again
to make sure
the box wouldn't tip
and then mounted the bike
and steered carefully
toward town,
staying in the hard-packed ruts
where pedaling was easier.

A story by Allan W. Eckert,
water colors by Willi Baum

Inside this box was the fruit
of his labors for two months—
forty-four prime pelts,
all properly stretched.
Some were not yet fully dry,
but Mr. Jensen wouldn't mind.
The local fur buyer
always stored them until March
before shipping them off
to New York, anyway.
He frowned, trying to figure
how much he'd get for them.
With twenty-two muskrats,
six raccoons, four skunks,
a gray fox, and eleven opossums,
it ought to come to about $80.
He whistled aloud, surprised.

   The trapping season
wasn't half over, either.
Last year when Rick Stephens
trapped with him,
their income for the whole season
was just $85...
and that hadn't been bad at all
for a pair of eleven-year-olds.
But this year the stone
had made it possible already
for him to buy
the two-skin choker he had seen
his mother stop to dream about
while leafing through a catalog.
The skins, of course, wouldn't be
from mink trapped by him,
as he had at first planned,
but at least they'd be
the *result* of his trapping.

   He was still a mile
from town when he saw

the tracks crossing the road
in front of him,
and he almost lost control
as he skidded to a stop.
The size of the toe tracks
and sweep of the tail
in the snow meant
it was a big cock pheasant.
A flush of excitement filled him.
These tracks were so new
that the falling snow hadn't even
begun to fill them,
and he was sure
it would take only a few minutes
to track the bird
to where it stopped.
What fun it would be
to flush out the big bird
and to imagine himself
shooting it and bringing it home
for dinner.
   He wheeled his bicycle
off the road,
braced it against a tree,
and kicked the front tire gently
to make sure
it wouldn't tip over
and dump the furs.
Keyed to a high pitch,
he followed the tracks
through the fence
into a woodlot,
then out the other side
and into an old soybean field.
He walked several hundred yards,
watching the tracks far ahead,
and then he saw them disappear
into a little mound of grass.

Tom licked his lips
and reached into his pocket
to rub his stone for luck.
He was dismayed
to find it gone.
Then he remembered
he had left it
in his other trousers
this morning.

Bothered
because he'd forgotten it,
he crept low over the snow
toward the bird's hiding place.
He was still ten feet away
when the pheasant burst
into the air
with a frightened screech
and rocketed away
on drumming wings.

"Would've got you if I had my stone!"
Tom shouted, peeved.
   He retraced his steps,
thinking about the big bird,
but when he crawled through the fence
at the edge of the woodlot,
he stopped as if he'd been struck.
The bicycle still leaned against the tree,
but the box was gone...the box and the furs.

In a daze he walked to the bike.
There were big marks in the snow—
the prints of a man—
coming from the road and returning there,
then disappearing at a new set of auto tracks.
The neatly cut ends of the rope hung silently
from the back carrier.
A moan of despair escaped him.
He felt sick as he returned home.
It was as if he had watched helplessly
as someone stole from his mother,
for the furs were really hers.
The great and wonderful Christmas gift
was now wholly impossible.
He ground his teeth and knew
that this would not have happened
if he had brought along his lucky stone.

Back in his room
he sat dejectedly
on his bed,
his hand clenched
around the stone.
He had nothing now to give,
nor was there time
to find some kind of job
to make enough money
for a present.
The stone felt warm
and smooth in his hand,
and tears filled his eyes
as he thought of the luck
it had brought him
since August.
    It was only natural
that it would become
his good luck piece
when he had found it.
He and Rick Stephens
had been clattering
down the rocky creek bed
when the brightness of it
caught his eye.

"Hey, boy! Look at this!"
he'd exclaimed, picking it up.

"Just an old chunk of rock," Rick said, sniffing,
peeved because he hadn't seen it first.
"Not near as big as my doorknob."

Rick had faithfully carried his brass doorknob
ever since they'd seen the *Tom Sawyer* movie together.
He had carefully polished away all trace of rust
until now the stemless knob gleamed like a fine lump of gold.
Tom had wanted a good luck piece like that more than anything,
and he searched for one everywhere—
even had his mother looking—
but unbattered doorknobs were hard to come by.

"Maybe so," he'd said,
"but I betcha you've never seen a chunk as neat as this one before.
It won't be so big to lug around in my pocket, either,
like that old doorknob of yours.
This is a real *natural* lucky piece.
Anybody can get a doorknob."

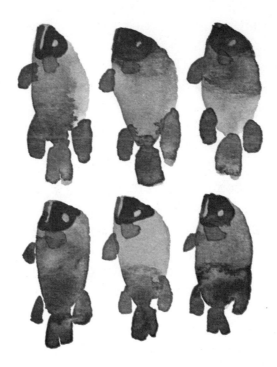

If the conversation had not taken such a turn,
Tom would probably have tried to trade
the shiny stone for the doorknob,
but now each of the boys had pledged himself
and a trade was impossible.
And, for a fact,
the stone did somehow seem to change Tom's luck.
When they finally reached
the fishing hole that day,
Tom caught seven bass, big ones,
while Rick caught only one little sunfish.

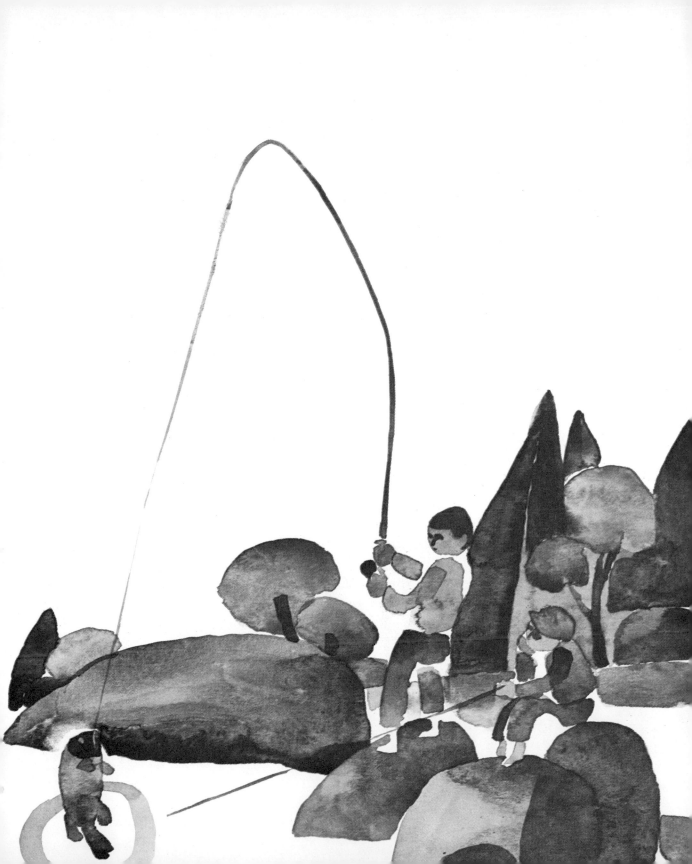

The good luck
brought by the stone—
it *had* to be the stone, Tom knew—
continued through the late summer.
When he entered seventh grade
in September,
it even seemed to help him there
because his teacher
was much better than last year's,
and somehow
the lessons came easier
and his grades were better.
Tom's mother, Mary Gentry,
had admired the stone
when Tom had shown it to her,
but she gently warned her son
not to count on good luck
to carry him through school.
And she had smiled when,
on the eve of the opening
of the trapping season,
Tom, sprawled on the floor,
carefully checked
over his twenty steel traps.
In turn he kissed the stone
and then touched it to the jaws
of each trap.
"That's to bring the luck
I'm going to need, Mom,"
he explained,
but her answering smile
was secretive.

He knew she thought he wanted to get lots of furs
to make extra money for himself,
but this year was going to be different.
This year the stone would help him catch the sixteen mink
necessary to have a stole made up for her Christmas present.
The fact that in the past three seasons of trapping with Rick,
he had never caught one, although Rick had caught two,
did not stop him.
After all, now that he had the lucky stone,
things would be different.
   For once, however, the good fortune hadn't come as planned.
True, he had wonderful luck catching other fur-bearers,
but he caught no mink. He refused to blame the stone.

If there were no mink around,
the stone couldn't do the impossible.

November dwindled and became a howling, snow-filled December.
Each morning, two hours before school, Tom arose
and ran his trapline. Whatever he caught he'd carry home
and then skin it and stretch the hide after school.
But the dream of a fine self-caught mink stole gradually dwindled
to that of a four-skin choker, also self-caught,
and finally just to a single, nicely tanned mink pelt
as an unusual gift for her.
Then it had become too late even for that,
and so Tom had made the plan to sell those hides he had caught
and buy the catalog choker.

And now ... now the whole effort
had been wasted and he had nothing to give.
He opened his hand
and looked at the stone carefully.
It was about the size of a pigeon egg
and very smooth. He breathed a faint mist on it,
polished it on his sleeve.
   "If I ever needed some good luck
and a good idea, I need it now," he said to the stone.
He held it to his lips for a moment,
but it slipped from his fingers
and caught for an instant in his shirtfront
just above a button, then fell to his lap.
But that brief pause had given him
the idea he needed.
The lucky stone was still lucky!
   An hour later he stood nervously
in front of the counter at Belden's Jewelry Store.
The old jeweler removed the lens
from his squinting eye as he listened to the boy's story.
He clucked his tongue sympathetically
when Tom told about missing the pheasant,
but his shaggy brows squinched down in a deep frown
when he heard about the stolen furs.
   "A dirty shame, that's what it is, Tom,"
he grumbled. "Feller's got to hang
onto his storebought teeth
or somebody'd swipe 'em sure.
No idea who took 'em?"
   "No, sir. I guess it could've been anyone.
I didn't see him. Didn't even hear him."

"Well," Fred Belden sighed, "I'm sorry for you,
but I can't quite figure why you've come
an' told me about it."

Tom dropped his eyes and fidgeted.
"I . . . I told you about my lucky stone.
It's awful pretty and I want to know
how much it'll cost to have it fixed up
sort of like a necklace."

"A necklace?"

"Well no, not exactly.
I mean like on a little gold chain that I can give
to my mother for Christmas,
and it'll hang down in front all by itself."

"Ah. You mean a pendant."

"Yes, sir."

"Oh," Belden looked at the boy and smiled.
"I suppose I could fix it up for you
for about ten dollars.
Most of that'd be for the gold chain itself."
When the boy neither spoke nor looked up,
the jeweler cleared his throat.
"How much money you got, Tom?"

"None, Mr. Belden. I thought . . . well,
I thought maybe after Christmas is over,
you might let me come down and work it off.
You know, like sweeping up and washing windows
and delivering and stuff like that."

Belden nodded his grizzled head.
"I guess we could do that all right.
Suppose I pay you two dollars a day
for five straight Saturdays. That suit you?"

"Yes, sir! That'd be fine."

"All right. You give me the stone and come back for it
just before closing time on Christmas Eve.
I'll have it all ready for you then in a nice box.
And you can start working the first Saturday after Christmas."

Tom nodded and dug in his pocket for the stone.
He cupped it in his hand for a moment
and then suddenly dropped it on the counter
and dashed out without another word.

Christmas morning dawned the way most people wish it would—
with a fresh layer of snow blanketing the world outside.

The large feathery snow clusters drifted earthward slowly,
and the spruce tree in the Gentry yard had miraculously become
a modernistic snowman. Mary Gentry stood at the window,
her arm about her son's shoulder.

"Beautiful, isn't it, Tom?"

"Uh, huh." He squeezed her hand.
"Merry Christmas, Mother."

"Come on," she said.
"Let's see what's in those beautiful packages under the tree."

Beneath the tree on the old sheet
spread out around the trunk to look like snow were the packages.
Mary Gentry smiled, nodding for Tom to begin opening his.

The first of his three packages
was a pair of woolen mittens
with a leather-lined slit
at each palm through which
he could slip his fingers
in order to do things
without having
to remove them entirely.
The second
was a rebuilt fishing reel,
much better than his old one,
and a spool of new line.
The third package was smallest,
and a new excitement filled him
when he opened it and saw
the shiny brass doorknob.

Then it was her turn,
and Tom watched eagerly
as she opened
the beautifully wrapped box
he had gotten from Mr. Belden
when he went into the store
yesterday.
Inside the cardboard box
was a smaller,
gray felt-covered box
with a hinged lid.
Her eyes widened,
and she sucked in her breath
as she opened it.
There,
on a cushion of red velvet,
was a very fine gold chain
to which was attached,
with a gold cap, the lucky stone.

Wordlessly,
she lifted it out,
looked at it
for a long quiet time
and then opened the clasp
and put it around her neck.
It had turned out beautifully
and appeared to glow
with an inner fire
as it caught and reflected
the lights from the little tree.
"Oh, Tom," she said at last.
"Tom. It's beautiful.
Just beautiful."
"It's a lucky piece, Mom,"
he said.
"If you wear it,
it'll bring you luck.
I had Mr. Belden
fix it up like this.
I wanted to give you
something else, but somebody...
something happened
and I couldn't.
But this'll bring you luck."
"How could it possibly
make me any luckier
than I am?" she asked softly.
She leaned over
and kissed his cheek
with great tenderness.
"I'm already the luckiest
mother in the world."
"And the best,"
the boy added seriously.

He picked up the fishing reel,
and his eyes were seeing slow-running creeks
and bright blue lakes as he cocked his head
to listen to the precision clicking
as he turned the handle.
"I think I'll put the line on it right now."

"All right," she said.
"I'll fix breakfast while you do. And Tom..."
He looked up. "Thank you for the beautiful pendant.
I know what it meant to you,
and I'll always treasure it."

She kissed the top of his head
and started into the kitchen, but the telephone rang
and she detoured to pick it up.

"Mrs. Gentry? Merry Christmas!
This is Fred Belden."

"Why, Mr. Belden. How nice of you to call.
Merry Christmas to you, too."

"I was wondering,"
the jeweler said slowly, carefully,
"if you and Tom have opened your gifts yet?"

"Why, yes, we have.
That was such a beautiful job you did
in mounting Tom's stone." She laughed lightly.
"He says it will bring me luck."

"Considerably more luck than you realize,
Mrs. Gentry," Belden said seriously.
"Like Tom, I thought it was just a pretty rock
until I got a closer look at it.
But it's more than just rock, a lot more.
It's a sapphire."

"Sapphire!"

"Yes. One of the finest I've seen.
Weighed exactly 28.72 carats.
Green-blue in color and flawless,
so far as I could detect.

Cut properly and polished, it should make a stone worth $2,000
or more. I'm prepared to pay you $1,700 for it as it is.
Or, if you wish, I'll have it sent to New York
to be cut and polished for you."

There was a long pause before Mary Gentry spoke softly.
"Thank you, Mr. Belden, but I think not.
You see, even though Tom didn't know what it really was,
it was something very dear to him.
So dear that it was a sacrifice for him to give it up.
It's very dear to me now, too, just the way it is—
not as a sapphire, but as a Christmas gift from my son.

"Oh, it's not that we couldn't use the money," she continued.
"With Tom's father gone, it's pretty hard most of the time,
but we've managed to make out well enough so far and we still will.
Someday I'll give this back to Tom
to help him get a college education."

"With a mother like you, Mrs. Gentry," Belden said,
"Tom doesn't need a stone for luck.
It is a merry Christmas, isn't it?"

A SONG For New Year

Should auld acquaintance[1] be forgot,
   And never brought to mind?
Should auld acquaintance be forgot
   And days of auld lang syne.[2]

For auld lang syne, my dear,
   For auld lang syne.
We'll tak' a cup o' kindness[3] yet,
   For auld lang syne.

[1]old friends
[2]days of long ago
[3]We'll drink a toast to days
  of long ago.

Poem by Robert Burns,
Lettering by Frank Aloise

Have you wondered what the last minutes are like just before take-off into space? Here's your chance to find out.

SPACE SHIP BIFROST

A story by Robert A. Heinlein, with drawings by Mel Hunter

I woke up hungry
but I suddenly remembered
that this was it!——
my last day on Earth.
Then I was too excited
to be hungry.
I got up,
put on my Scout uniform
and my ship suit over it.
I thought we would go
right on board,
I was wrong.
First we had to assemble
under awnings
spread out in front of the hotel
near the embarking tubes.
It wasn't air-conditioned outside,
of course,
but it was early
and the desert
wasn't really hot yet.
I found the letter *L*
and sat down under it,
sitting on my baggage.
Dad and his new family
weren't around yet:
What could be keeping them?
I began to wonder
if I was going to *Ganymede*[1]
by myself.
I didn't much care.
I wasn't very fond
of all my new family.

Out past the gates,
about five miles away,
you could see the ships
standing on the field.

[1]pronounced găn' ē mēd

The *Daedalus*[2] and the *Icarus*[3]
had been pulled off
the Earth-Moon run
for this one trip,
as had the old *Bifrost*
that had been the shuttle rocket
to Supre-New York space station
as far back
as I could remember.
The *Daedalus* and the *Icarus*
were bigger,
but I hoped
I would get the *Bifrost;*
she was the first ship
I ever saw blast off.
A family put their baggage down
by mine.
The mother looked out
across the field
and said,
"Joseph,
which one is the *Mayflower?*"
Her husband tried
to explain to her,
but she still was puzzled.
I nearly burst,
trying to keep from laughing.
Here she was,
all set to go to *Ganymede*
and yet she was so dumb
she didn't even know
that the ship she was going in
had been built out in space
and couldn't land anywhere.[4]

[2]pronounced *dĕd' ə ləs*
[3]pronounced *ik' ər əs*
[4]A ship like this, one which has no point of
landing, is called a *space-to-space* ship. It
was built out in space and always will remain
there.

The place was getting crowded
with emigrants and relatives
coming to see them off,
but I still didn't see
anything of Dad.
I heard my name called
and turned around,
and there was Duck Miller.

"Gee, Bill," he said,
"I thought I'd missed you."

"Hi, Duck.
No, I'm still here."

"I tried to call you last night
but your phone answered
'service discontinued,'
so I hooked school and came up."

"Aw, you shouldn't have done that."

"But I wanted to bring you this."
He handed me a package,
a whole pound of chocolates.
I didn't know what to say.
I thanked him and then said,
"Duck, I appreciate it,
I really do.
But I'll have to give them
back to you."

"Huh? Why?"

"Weight. Mass, I mean.
I can't get by
with another ounce."

"You can carry it."

"That won't help.
It counts just the same."
He thought about it and said,
"Then let's open it."
I said, "Fine,"
and did so
and offered him a piece.
I looked at them myself,
and my stomach
was practically sitting up
and begging.
I don't know
when I've been so hungry.
I gave in
and ate one.
I figured
I would sweat it off anyhow;
it was getting hot,
and I had my Scout uniform on
under my ship suit —
and that's no way to dress
for the Mojave[5] Desert in June!
Then I was thirstier than ever,
of course;
one thing leads to another.
I went over to a drinking fountain
and took a very small drink.

When I came back,
I closed the candy box
and handed it back to Duck
and told him to pass it around
at the next Scout meeting
and tell the fellows
I wished they were going along.

He said he would
and added,

"You know, Bill,
I wish I was going,
I really do."
I said I wished he was too,
but when did he change his mind?
He looked embarrassed,
but about then
Mr. Kinski showed up,
and then Dad showed up,
with Molly and the brat —
Peggy —
and Molly's sister,
Mrs. van Metre.[6]
Everybody shook hands
all around,
and Mrs. van Metre started to cry
and *the brat* wanted to know
what made my clothes so bunchy
and what was I sweating about?
George was eyeing me,
but about then
our names were called
and we started moving
through the gate.
George and Molly and Peggy
were weighed through,
and then it was my turn.

My baggage was right on the nose,
of course,
and then I stepped on the scales.
They read
one hundred and thirty-one
and one-tenth pounds ——
I could have eaten
another chocolate.

[5]pronounced *Mō hä' vē*

[6]Only a family with the name of van Metre
could decide how it should be pronounced in
English. They would, at least, have the choice
of *van Mē'-tər* or *van Mē-trə.*

"Check!" said the weightmaster;
  then he looked up and said,
"What in the world
  have you got on, son?"
The left sleeve of my uniform
had started to unroll
and was sticking out
below the half sleeve
of my ship suit.
The merit badges[7]
were shining out
like signal lights.
I didn't say anything.
He started feeling the lumps
the uniform sleeves made.
"Boy," he said,
"you're dressed
  like an Arctic explorer;
no wonder you're sweating.
Didn't you know
you weren't supposed to wear
anything but the gear
you were listed in?"

[7]Boy Scouts receive *merit badges* for per-
forming certain tasks or passing certain tests.

Dad came back
and asked what the trouble was.
I just stood there
with my ears burning.
The assistant weightmaster
got into the huddle,
and they argued
about what should be done.
The weightmaster phoned somebody
and finally he said,
"He's inside his weight limit;
if he wants to call
that monkey suit
part of his skin,
we'll allow it.
Next customer, please!"

I trailed along, feeling foolish.
We went down inside
and climbed on the slide strip;
it was cool down there,
thank goodness.
A few minutes later
we got off at the loading room
down under the rocket ship.
Sure enough, it was the *Bifrost*,
as I found out
when the loading elevator
poked above ground
and stopped at the passenger port.
We filed in.
They had it all organized.
Our baggage had been taken from us
in the loading room;
each passenger had a place
assigned by his weight.

That split us up again;
I was on the deck
immediately under
the control room.
I found my place, couch 14-D,
then went to a view port
where I could see
the *Daedalus* and the *Icarus*.

A brisk little stewardess,
about knee-high to a grasshopper,
checked my name off a list
and offered me an injection
against dropsickness.
I said no, thanks.

She said,
"You've been out before?"

I admitted I hadn't.

She said, "Better take it."

I said
I was a licensed air pilot;
I wouldn't get sick.
I didn't tell her
that my license
was just for 'copters.

She shrugged and turned away.

A loudspeaker said,
"The *Daedalus* is cleared
for blasting."
I moved up to get a good view.
The *Daedalus* was
about a quarter of a mile away
and stood up higher than we did.

She had fine lines
and was a mighty pretty sight,
gleaming in the morning sunshine.

Beyond her and to the right,
clear out at the edge of the field,
a light shone green
at the traffic control blockhouse.
She canted[8] slowly over to the south,
just a few degrees.

Fire burst out of her base,
orange, and then blinding white.
It splashed down
into the ground baffles[9]
and curled back up
through the ground vents.
She lifted.
She hung there for a breath,
and you could see the hills
shimmer through her jet.
And she was *gone!*
Just like that—she was *gone!*
She went up out of there
like a scared bird,

8Isn't it interesting that even though you may
not know the exact meaning of this word, you
get the sense of it by its use in the sentence
and can go on reading without stopping to
look it up.
9*baffles:* used to deflect fire

just a pencil of white fire
in the sky,
and was *gone*
while we could still hear and feel
the thunder of her jets
inside the compartment.
My ears were ringing.

I heard someone behind me
say,
"But I haven't had breakfast.
The Captain
will just have to wait.
Tell him, Joseph."

It was the woman
who hadn't known
that the *Mayflower*
was a space-to-space ship.
Her husband tried
to hush her up,
but he didn't have any luck.
She called over the stewardess.
I heard her answer,
"But, madam,
you can't speak
to the Captain now.
He's preparing for blast-off."

Apparently
that didn't make any difference.
The stewardess finally got her quiet
by solemnly promising
that she could have breakfast
after blast-off.
I bent my ears at that,
and I decided to put in
a bid for breakfast, too.

The *Icarus* took off
twenty minutes later,
and then the speaker said,
"All hands!
Acceleration stations[10] ——
prepare to blast off."

I went back to my couch
and the stewardess made sure
that we were all strapped down.
She cautioned us not to unstrap
until she said we could.
She went down
to the deck below.

I felt my ears pop,
and there was a soft sighing
in the ship.
I swallowed
and kept swallowing.
I knew what they were doing:
blowing the natural air out
and replacing it with
the standard helium-oxygen[11] mix
at half sea-level pressure.
But the woman — the same one —
didn't like it.

[10]Who knows what *acceleration stations* actually means in this sentence? No one, probably, but the author. It could mean, for example, that all hands were to go to their *acceleration stations*. Or it could mean for *all* acceleration station hands to be attentive to the command *prepare to blast off.*

[11]These are science terms that you may want to investigate. Isn't it interesting that you can get the meaning of the story without having to know the exact meaning of every specific term?

She said, "Joseph, my head aches.
Joseph, I can't breathe.
Do something!"
Then she clawed at her straps
and sat up.
Her husband sat up, too,
and forced her back down.
The *Bifrost* tilted over a little,
and the speaker said,
"Minus three minutes!"
After a long time it said,
"Minus two minutes!"
And then "Minus one minute!"
and another voice
took up the count:
"Fifty-nine!
Fifty-eight!
Fifty-seven!"
My head started to pound so hard
I could hardly hear it.
But it went on:
"——thirty-five!
Thirty-four!
Thirty-three!
Thirty-two!
Thirty-one!
Half!
Twenty-nine!
Twenty-eight!"

And it got to be: "Ten!"
And "Nine!
Eight!
Seven!"
And "Six!"
And "Five!"
And "Four!"
And "Three!"
And "Two—"

I never did hear them say
one or *fire*
or whatever they said.
About then
something fell on me,
and I thought I was licked.
Once, while I was exploring a cave
with the fellows,
a bank collapsed on me
and I had to be dug out.
It was like that —
but nobody dug me out.
My chest hurt.
My ribs seemed about to break.
I couldn't lift a finger.
I gulped
and couldn't get my breath.
I wasn't scared, not really,
because I knew we would take off
with a *high g*,[12]
but I was awfully uncomfortable.

I managed
to turn my head a little
and saw that the sky
was already purple.
While I watched,
it turned black
and the stars came out,
millions of stars.
And yet
the sun was still streaming in
through the port.
The roar of the jets
was unbelievable,
but the noise started to die out
almost at once,
and soon
you couldn't hear at all.

They say
the old ships used to be noisy
even after
you passed the speed of sound;
the *Bifrost* was not.
It got quiet
as the inside of a bag of feathers.

There was nothing to do
but lie there,
stare out at that black sky,
try to breathe,
and try not to think about
the weight sitting on you.

And then,
so suddenly
that it made your stomach
turn flip-flops,
you didn't weigh anything at all.

[12]The letter *g* is used by flyers and spacemen
to stand for the force of gravity. A *high g* is
many times greater than normal gravity.

SEPTEMBER

The golden-rod is yellow,
　　The corn is turning brown;
The trees in apple orchards
　　With fruit are bending down.

The gentian's bluest fringes
　　Are curling in the sun;
In dusty pods the milkweed
　　Its hidden silk has spun.

The sedges flaunt their harvest,
　　In every meadow-nook;
And asters by the brookside
　　Make asters in the brook.

By all these lovely tokens
　　September days are here,
With summer's best of wealth
　　And autumn's best of cheer.

A poem by Helen Hunt Jackson,
painting by Stanley Maltzman

Hopi
nake
Dance

Most of the Indian tribes
of the early American frontier
lived by hunting buffalo
and other animals.
These tribes were wanderers.
They were good hunters
and fierce warriors.

There were a few tribes,
however, that did not depend
on hunting as a means
of securing food.
These tribes made their living
by farming.
They wanted nothing more
than rain for their crops
and to till their fields
in peace.
One of these groups of farmers
was the Hopi Indian tribe
that lived and still lives
in Arizona and New Mexico.

Pictures by Ted Rand

58

The Hopis did not live in tepees
as the nomadic,[1]
hunting tribes did.
They lived
in large adobe[2] houses
called pueblos.
Many families lived
in each pueblo.
Their principal food was corn
which they grew
in communal[3] fields.

[1] wandering
[2] clay, bricklike
[3] shared by the entire community

Growing corn
was a difficult task.
The weather was hot and dry,
and there was little rainfall.
The earth in summer
turned to hot, powdery dust,
and the corn leaves withered
and browned on the stalks.
During such years
there was little or no harvest,
and the Hopis went hungry.
Consequently,
in some prehistoric time,
the Hopis devised a ritual[4]
called a *Snake Dance*
to entreat their god for rain.
Like many primitive people
of ancient times,
the Hopis believed
that a snake was a god
with the power to bring rainfall
and an abundant harvest of corn.
The Hopis of today
still perform the Snake Dance
as a prayer for rain
when the dry season approaches.

[4] religious ceremony

The Snake Dance today
is performed
in much the same manner
as it was
hundreds of years ago.
The major difference
is that today
people from outside the tribe
are permitted
to watch the ceremony.
Tourists come
from all over the world
to see this strange
and primitive ritual.
It takes place in August
of every other year
when the corn crop
is about half grown.

Four days before the dance,
a large group of Indian men,
dressed only in loincloths[5]
and moccasins,
go out into the desert
to hunt snakes.
The men are the Snake Priests
of the tribe.
These Snake Priests first go
to the west,
then to the south,
then to the east,
and finally to the north
in search for snakes.
Each priest carries
a jug of water,
a sack of cornmeal,

and two buzzard feathers.
The Hopis believe
that buzzard feathers have
a strange and powerful odor
that will soften
the anger of a snake
and allow it to be captured.

The Snake Priests
capture every snake they find,
whether it be bull snake,
racer, gopher snake, or rattler.
Most snakes have no defense
against man,
and therefore are not dangerous.
The rattlesnake, however,
when frightened or angry,
coils itself up like a spring
and prepares to strike
anybody who comes near
with its poisonous fangs.
A Snake Priest is careful,
therefore, when he approaches
a coiled and hissing rattlesnake.
He waves the buzzard feathers
over the snake,
and, strangely enough,
the buzzard feathers
have a quieting effect
on the snake.
In time the snake uncoils
and seems unafraid
of the Indian standing near.
Then, quickly and carefully,
the Snake Priest
grabs the rattlesnake
behind its head.

[5] cloths worn loosely around
the waist to drape the loins

The snake thrashes about
in the air,
trying to get loose,
but the Snake Priest holds fast.
The priest then spits
into the palm of his free hand
and, with his wet palm,
brushes the snake
down the length of its body
over and over again.
This motion either soothes
or hypnotizes the snake,
for soon it stops fighting
and hangs limply
like a piece of rope
in the priest's hand.

The snake is placed in a bag
and carried back to the pueblo
to be used
in the Snake Dance ceremony.

Four days of hunting
usually produce
about sixty snakes
of all kinds and sizes.
The snakes are kept in jars
and are blessed with cornmeal.
Each evening after dark,
the Snake Priests
entertain the snakes.
The priests sit cross-legged
on the ground in a tight circle
around the jars of snakes.
Then the snakes are released.
As the snakes begin
to slither about
in the circle,
the priests sing to them
in soft, low voices.
The snakes seem unafraid.
They approach the priests
and often crawl into their laps.
The Snake Priests do not move
or show fear.
On the contrary,
each priest hopes
that many snakes will crawl
into his lap
because he believes
that the snakes only come
to a priest with a pure heart.

He considers it an honor
to be visited by a snake.

The entertainment of the snakes
lasts all night.
The priests sing
to the snakes until dawn.
Then the snakes are put back
into the jars,
and the priests go to the spring
to bathe themselves.
The bathing is part of the ritual.

The fifth day
is the day of the Snake Dance.

All the captured snakes
are placed in a pit
in the pueblo square.
Cottonwood planks
are placed over the pit
to keep the snakes from escaping.
The planks also act
as a "drum" on which
the dancers stomp loudly.

At the beginning of the dance,
the Snake Priests
blacken their faces.

They paint their chests
and their arms.
Then they dance
into the pueblo square
to the loud beat of drums.
As the priests
pass over the snake pit,
they stomp their feet
on the cottonwood planks,
producing a sound
like the dull rumble
of distant thunder.
The Hopis pray
that the sounds from the pit
will soon be echoed
by the sounds of real thunder
in the sky.
The rest of the Indians
of the pueblo
gather around the dancers
to join in the prayer for rain
by beating drums
and chanting songs.

Soon the Chief Snake Priest
lifts a plank off the snake pit
and grabs a snake
from the writhing mass
within the pit.
He puts the snake in his mouth,
holding it behind the head
with his teeth.
He takes the snake's body
in his hands
and holds it in the shape
of an *S*
as he begins to dance
around the pueblo square.
The drums beat louder,
and the chanting increases.

Then a second Snake Priest
goes to the pit.
He, like the first priest,
takes a snake in his mouth
and joins the dance
around the circle.
He is soon followed

by a third priest,
a fourth, a fifth, and so on,
until all the priests
are dancing with snakes
held between their teeth.
As each Snake Priest
dances the full circle
with a snake,
he hands that snake
to his assistant
and returns to the pit
to pick up another snake.
By the end of the ritual,
each of the sixty snakes
has been danced with
and handled.

As the dance
builds to its climax,
one of the small boys
of the pueblo
rushes into the square
and takes a snake in his mouth.
He joins the dancing priests
in their prayer for rain.
If the elders approve of him,
he may someday
be invited to become
one of the Snake Priests
of the tribe.

When the dance is finished,
the Snake Priests carry
all the captured snakes
back to their homes
in the hot, dry desert,
where they are released.
The Snake Dance ceremony
for that year is over.

The Snake Priests
return to the pueblo,
and their women help them
remove the paint
from their bodies.
Then all the Indians
of the pueblo
sit down to a feast of cornmeal.
As they eat,
they listen for the rumble
of distant thunder
to tell them that
the "magic" of the Snake Dance
has worked
and that raindrops
will soon be falling
on the fields of corn.

SPRING
**Haiku by Soseki,
painting by Chen Chi**

Little silver fish pointing upstream
Moving downstream in clear quick water

SUMMER
**Haiku by Shiki,
painting by Chen Chi**

What a splendid day! No one in all
The village doing anything!

AUTUMN
Haiku by Shiki,
painting by Chen Chi

Nights are getting cold. Not a single insect
Now attacks the candle

WINTER
by Bill Martin, Jr.,
painting by Chen Chi

The snowy day that closed the schools
Opened the doors to let children out.

A Birthday

My heart is like a singing bird
   Whose nest is in a watered shoot:
My heart is like an apple-tree
   Whose boughs are bent with thickset fruit;
My heart is like a rainbow shell
   That paddles in a halcyon sea;
My heart is gladder than all these
   Because my love is come to me.

Raise me a dais of silk and down;
   Hang it with vair and purple dyes;
Carve it in doves and pomegranates,
   And peacocks with a hundred eyes;
Work it in gold and silver grapes,
   In leaves and silver fleurs-de-lys;
Because the birthday of my life
   Is come, my love is come to me.

A poem by Christina Rossetti,
illustrated by Betty Fraser

HENRY REED, INC.

A story by Keith Robertson,
with illustrations by Robert McCloskey

Henry Harris Reed comes from Italy to spend
the summer with an aunt and uncle in New Jersey.
His teacher in the American school in Naples —
where his father is United States consul—has asked
him to keep notes on his experiences and, if possible, to "do something that can be used to illus-
trate free enterprise." Little does she know what
a chain of reactions she has touched off!

This book is Henry's private journal (*not* a diary
—"diaries are kept by girls"), in which he gravely
records the sidesplitting details of his undertakings.
To begin with, he tidies up an old barn and paints
a sign on the outside:

HENRY REED,
RESEARCH

Watching him at work, Margaret Glass, the girl next door, says he should add "Pure and Applied" before the word "Research." Henry has a poor opinion of girls in general, but as a businessman he realizes that Margaret knows more or less what she is talking about and just *might* be useful as a partner.

Eventually the sign reads

REED & GLASS, INC.
Pure and Applied Research

But before that time comes, a great many people —not to speak of an assortment of animals—have been entangled in an astonishing series of enterprises that could only be called "free"!

Drawings by Robert McCloskey—famous author-artist of the hilarious *Homer Price* and *Centerburg Tales* — add the perfect complement of humor to situations in the journal that are sometimes mysterious, often profitable, and always wildly funny.

Monday, July 29th

I have half a notion to write the postmaster general and tell him what I think of the way the mail is being handled at Grover's Corner. I suppose most rural mail carriers are pretty nice people, but the one who delivers the mail to us isn't very cooperative or very intelligent for that matter. Of course, from the things he said, I guess he doesn't think much of Midge or me either, so things are about balanced.

For the past two or three days we haven't had even one rabbit. Midge had the idea that if we let Mathilda out of the pen to run loose, she might decoy Jedidiah back with her.

"And she might get as wild as he is," I objected.

"Not if we don't leave her out too long," Midge said. "I've let her go several times, and she lets me walk right up to her."

I finally agreed, because one rabbit alone isn't much good when you want to raise rabbits to sell. Anyhow, we let Mathilda out. Midge was right; at first she was able to walk up to the rabbit without much trouble. For a while it looked as if the scheme might work. That evening, about dusk, Mathilda came hopping up to the pen, and Jedidiah was with her. We had left one end of the pen open, and the plan was to wait until they were both inside eating, and then to slip up and close the opening. Jedidiah went inside, and he seemed hungry. However, he wasn't so hungry that he forgot to keep an eye on us. Midge was within three feet of the pen when he bolted out and ran for the tree.

We left the pen open, and I suppose Mathilda hopped back out after she had eaten. We saw them several times yesterday, but we didn't get very close. I don't know whether Mathilda had decided she liked freedom too or was just following Jedidiah, but she hopped away too. Midge began to get worried.

"He's a bad influence," she said. "I should never have let Mathilda go out with him."

This morning about ten-thirty, as I was walking toward the lot, I saw both rabbits beneath a rose bush in the Millers' front yard. I hurried to the barn to get a net and then over to get Midge for help. She got her father's fishing net and came along.

Both rabbits were facing the same way, and I don't know whether they were dozing or not, but we crept up quietly until we were only a few feet behind them. They didn't move. We have had a lot of practice trying to catch Jedidiah with a hand net, so I suppose we had to do it right sooner or later. We both pounced at once. Our timing was perfect, and Midge got one rabbit and I got the other.

"Hurrah! I'm a member of the firm!" Midge shouted.

I had caught Mathilda and Midge had Jedidiah. I reached in and got Mathilda by the nape of the neck and pulled her out of the net, kicking and squirming like mad. A big rabbit like that is not easy to hold. Finally I got her cradled in my left arm, still holding onto the loose skin of her neck with my right hand. Then she quieted down.

Midge had a much rougher time. Jedidiah was wild, and he wasn't giving up without a fight. He kicked and ripped a hole in the net. Afraid that he would ruin the net, Midge lifted him out. He came out easily enough, but then he really began acting up. Her arms were bare, and in a couple of seconds he had scratched her left arm so badly in several places that it was all over blood.

"I can't hold him much longer," she said. "What will I do?"

We were standing beside the **Millers'** mailbox. Grover's Corner is on a rural mail route, and everyone has sheet-metal mailboxes on posts out beside the road. The Millers' mailbox is a big one, and suddenly it occurred to me that we could use it.

"Stuff him in there," I suggested.

Midge yanked open the mailbox, shoved Jedidiah inside, and slammed the lid shut again. The lid fits tightly, so we weren't worried about the rabbit getting out. Carrying Mathilda, we headed back toward the barn.

We had to close the end of Mathilda's pen before we put her in it, and then we went over to Midge's to locate something to use in carrying Jedidiah back. We weren't satisfied with an ordinary pasteboard box because we didn't want to take any chances. Finally we found an old peach basket with a lid.

We were gone about five minutes. When we got in sight of the mailbox again, we saw a Willys Jeep station wagon belonging to the mailman parked in front of it.

"Don't open the mailbox!" we both shouted, and we started running down the road.

We were too late. Mr. Mason, the mailman, opened the mailbox just as we yelled. He had driven up close to the box. He rolled down his car window and opened the lid. He was about to shove some letters in the box when the rabbit jumped out, practically in his face.

Since the open car window was only about a foot away, naturally Jedidiah went right through it. He landed half on the steering wheel and then tumbled into Mr. Mason's lap.

The rabbit wasn't as surprised as Mr. Mason, and he recovered sooner. He scrambled out of Mason's lap and onto the seat beside him. Mr. Mason had a big pile of letters stretched out on the seat, all arranged according to his route. What that rabbit did to that mail shouldn't happen to anyone. It was scattered all over the seat and floor as though a hurricane had hit it. Then Jedidiah jumped into the back, which was filled with packages and still more mail.

Mr. Mason let out a bellow and lunged over the seat after him. By this time I was standing at one front window looking in, and Midge was at the other. There was a mad scramble in the back of the station wagon, with letters flying and packages sliding every which way. Jedidiah raced around like a crazy rabbit while Mr. Mason flailed around after him. Finally Mason made a dive and came up holding the rabbit by his ears.

"You caught him," Midge shouted. "Good for you. I'll take him."

Mr. Mason climbed back over the front seat, puffing and red-faced. Still holding the rabbit by the ears, he shoved him through the open front window. I was hurrying around the front of the car to Midge's side because I had the basket. Before I got there, the rabbit doubled up his hind legs and kicked. Two long red scratches appeared on Mr. Mason's arm. He gave a bellow of pain and let the rabbit drop. Midge tried to catch him, but she didn't get a good grip. The rabbit gave a mighty kick and shot out of her hands into the bushes.

"Why'd you drop him?" Midge demanded.

"Because the vicious little beast was ripping me to pieces," Mason said angrily, looking at his arm.

"Now we'll never get him," Midge said disappointedly. "You might at least have held him a second longer."

"If you think you've got troubles, look at this car," Mason said. "I spent two hours sorting that mail, and now look at it. Well, you two can tell anybody that asks that this route is going to be mighty late in getting its mail today." He glared at the scattered mail. "Two hours' work wasted!"

"We've had weeks of work wasted," I said. "That's how long we've been chasing that rabbit."

"Well, you certainly picked a fine place to put him when you did catch him," Mason said.

"We just put him there until we could get back with this basket," I said.

"He was a male rabbit," Midge said very innocently.

For a minute I thought Mr. Mason was going to explode. Then he put his hands on the edge of the window and leaned part way through. He stuck his jaw out and said, "If I find that male rabbit in another mailbox, I'll stamp him, and good!"

The Chickamungus

A poem by James Reeves,
illustration by Jim Spanfeller

All in the groves of dragon-fungus
Lives the mysterious Chickamungus.
The natives who inhabit there
Have never yet found out his lair;
And if by chance they did, no doubt
The Chickamungus would be out.
For he is seldom found at home;
He likes to rove, he likes to roam.
He never sleeps but what he snores,
He never barks but what he roars,
He never creeps but what he walks,
He never climbs but what he stalks,
He never trots but what he hobbles,
He never stands but what he wobbles,
He never runs but what he skims,
He never flies but what he swims.
At tom-tom time he romps and roves
Among the odorous dragon-groves.
He lives on half-grown formicoots
And other sorts of roots and shoots.
He has been seen at rest among
His multitudinivorous young;
And travelers returning late
Have heard him crying for his mate.
His tracks have been identified,
Straying a bit from side to side,
Across the desert plains of Quunce.
A native girl observed him once,
But could not say what she had seen,
So unobservant had she been.
Her evidence is inconclusive,
And so the beast remains elusive.
A naturalist who found his den
Was never after seen again.
Thus we must leave the Chickamungus
At large amidst the dragon-fungus.

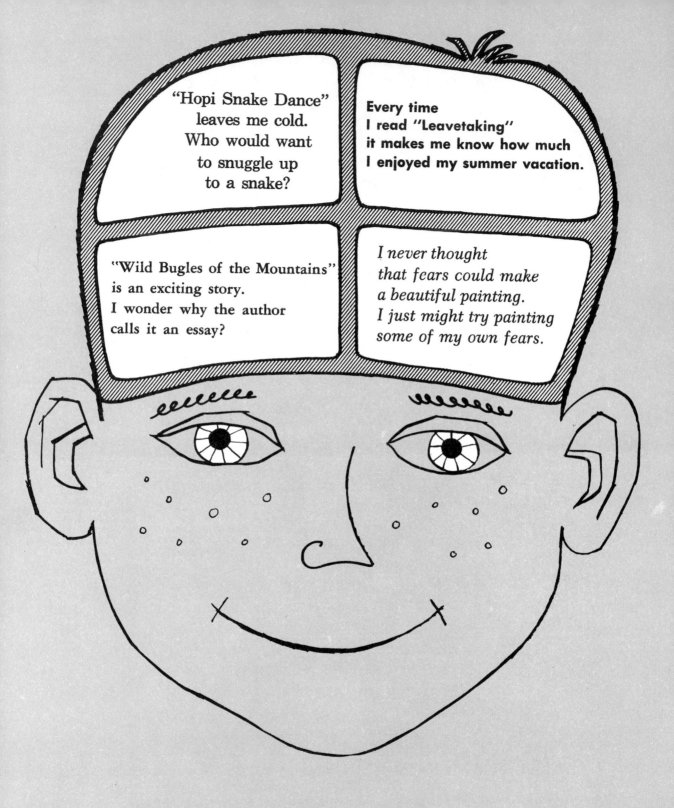

"Hopi Snake Dance"
leaves me cold.
Who would want
to snuggle up
to a snake?

Every time
I read "Leavetaking"
it makes me know how much
I enjoyed my summer vacation.

"Wild Bugles of the Mountains"
is an exciting story.
I wonder why the author
calls it an essay?

I never thought
that fears could make
a beautiful painting.
I just might try painting
some of my own fears.

viewing the printed page

I will always remember
an experience in a first grade,
once, when Peter asked me
to tell him the "story"
about the end of the world.
"What story is that?" I asked.
I couldn't recall any story
of that sort for first-graders.
"It's the one you told my brother
when he was in the first grade,"
Peter said.
"You know, the one
where the world burns up."
Then I recollected
the "story" (poem)
that Peter's brother had liked
over and over again:

FIRE AND ICE
Some say the world will end in fire,
Some say in ice.
From what I've tasted of desire
I hold with those who favor fire.
But if it had to perish twice,
I think I know enough of hate
To say that for destruction ice
Is also great
And would suffice.
by Robert Frost

Isn't it something of a miracle,
first, that Peter's brother
loved that poem so much
that he could recite it
to his small brother
and, second,
that Peter himself
remembered the poem
and wanted to hear it spoken again?
I watched Peter's face
as I repeated the poem,
and I sensed that Peter
was being deeply stirred
by the beauty of the poem
and its intriguing use of language.
For Peter,
the poem was an art experience.
It would not surprise me
to know that he,
much older now,
is saying the same poem today
for his own pleasure
  and satisfaction.
He probably will be repeating it
for a lifetime,
each time with joy and wondering.
This is the way it is with art.
It gets inside of you.
It causes you to feel *alive*.

as an art experience

An essay by Bill Martin, Jr.,
drawing by Frank Aloise

It puts you more in tune
with your dreams and feelings
and with things as they are.
It may not seem
to teach you anything,
but it makes you feel
more of a person
than you would have felt otherwise.

Now, let me invite you·
"behind the scenes"
into the planning of this book.
Sounds of a Distant Drum
is meant to give you
a wide exposure
to many of the kinds of things
that are art experiences to me.
I can't know
what they will be for you,
because each of us
responds differently
to pages of a book.
But every line of type
and every picture
and every selection in this book
was deliberately planned
so that you can discover
the artistic pleasure in reading.

Do you recognize, for example,
how many different techniques
the artists have used
in illustrating this book:
crayons, pencil drawings,

water colors, oil paints,
photographs, collage,
sculpture, wood carving, pen and ink?
Have any of these illustrations
had an effect on you?
Do you realize how many ways
the type has been arranged:
in narrow columns
with straight left and right margins;
in uneven lines that are broken
into patterns like people speak;
in circular and slanting shapes
that follow the art on the page;
in large and small typefaces
to suggest different sounds;
in measured accented lines
to catch the feel of poetry?
Have any of these type arrangements
had any effect on you?
And how about the language itself?

Did
All in the groves of dragon-fungus
Lives the mysterious Chickamungus.
get in your "blood stream"?
And how about the picture
of the Chickamungus?
Turn back to page 80
and look at that drawing again.
Notice the flow of the flowers
in the background,
the overlapping softness
of the feathery body,
the candy-stripe colors of the tail.

Is this picture by Jim Spanfeller
one that you may be remembering
with pleasure forty years from now?
Or will it be forgotten tomorrow?

Which of the stories or poems
or articles that you have read
thus far in the book are ones
that you gave yourself to
with the feeling
that you had encountered
something important?
Have you flipped through the rest
of the book?
Do you see pages that intrigued you
and that you're looking forward
to reading?

You may have the notion
from what I've been saying
that every page in this book
is going to be a great revelation—
that every page has some magic
to make you come alive—
but that isn't how it is with art.
You may read
a hundred stories or poems
before you find one that gives you
that special feeling,
that special glimpse
into the worthwhileness of living.
You may encounter a hundred
paintings before one takes hold
of you, draws you into its being.

Once you have found a favorite,
oh! how satisfying.
It's then that you come to know
that the search
for special artistic experiences
is well worth the effort
and that your next find
may even change your mind
about some of the earlier
selections and rejections.
You may be asking,
"What does art experience
have to do with reading?"
I would answer, "Everything.
This is what reading is all about.
Reading is not simply
pronouncing words correctly,
nor is it looking at a picture
to name an object,
nor is it giving 'right answers'
to someone else's questions.
Reading is a way of putting
words and pictures and feelings
and ideas together
to help you know better who you are,
to help you feel better
about yourself,
to help you think better
in solving troublesome problems,
to help you be glad
that you're alive."
"Oh," but you say, "that's what
you just said about art experience."
"Yes," I answer. "Reading is art."

This picture of Indians on the move was painted by a distinguished contemporary artist, John Clymer. Have you ever stopped to think about these early trailblazers and the fact that the Indian was a pioneer?

The Pioneer

Long years ago I blazed a trail
    Through lovely woods unknown till then
And marked with cairns of splintered shale
    A mountain way for other men;

For other men who came and came:
    They trod the path more plain to see,
They gave my trail another's name
    And no one speaks or knows of me.

The trail runs high, the trail runs low
    Where windflowers dance or columbine;
The scars are healed that long ago
    My ax cut deep on birch and pine.

Another's name my trail may bear,
    But still I keep, in waste and wood,
My joy because the trail is there,
    My peace because the trail is good.

taken from *I Sing the Pioneer*, by Arthur Guiterman

FOOD, GLORIOUS FOOD! HOT SAUSAGE & MUSTARD! WHILE WE'RE IN THE MOOD.

Cold jelly and custard! Pease pudding and saveloys. "What next?" is the question. Rich gentlemen have it, boys — In-dye-ges-tion! Food, glorious food! We're anxious to try it. Three banquets a day—our favourite diet! Just picture a great big steak—Fried, roasted, or stewed. Oh, food, wonderful food, marvelous food, glorious food— What is it we dream about? What brings on a sigh? Piled peaches and cream about six feet high! Bring on the food, ma-gical food, won-derful food, mar-vel ous food, fa-bulous food,   BEAUTI

FUL FOOD,

GLORI

OUS FOOD,

WONDER

PEAS

I eat my peas with honey,
    I've done it all my life.
It makes the peas taste funny,
    But it keeps them on my knife.

Anonymous

FUL FOOD.

A Cock-eyed Optimist

When the sky is a bright canary yellow
I forget ev'ry cloud I've ever seen,
So they call me a cock-eyed optimist
Immature and incurably green.

I have heard people rant and rave and bellow
That we're done and we might as well be dead,
But I'm only a cock-eyed optimist
And I can't get it into my head.

I hear the human race
Is falling on its face
And hasn't very far to go,
But ev'ry whippoorwill
Is selling me a bill,
And telling me it just ain't so.

I could say life is just a bowl of jello
And appear more intelligent and smart,
But I'm stuck like a dope
With a thing called hope,
And I can't get it out of my heart!

Not this heart!

A song by Richard Rodgers and Oscar Hammerstein II

The Mist and All

Solo 1: *I like the fall,*
The mist and all.

Solo 2: *I like the night owl's*
Lonely call —

All: *And wailing sound*
Of wind around.

Solo 3: *I like the gray*
November day,

All: *And bare, dead boughs*
That coldly sway
Against my pane.

Solo 4: *I like the rain.*

Solo 5: *I like to sit*
And laugh at it —

All: *And tend*
My cozy fire a bit.

Solo 6: *I like the fall —*

All: *The mist and all.*

A poem by Dixie Willson,
picture by Ed Young

A Letter from the Artist

In illustrating "The Quail," the story which follows, I was asked to do four pictures. I conceived the pictures as a sequence showing character development — that is, showing the boy's character change from the beginning to the end. The story is clearly about a progression from boy to man, a coming of age—in effect, the Loss of Innocence.

The first painting identifies the hunting situation and puts it in an idyllic setting, a boyhood Elysium of natural beauty and goodness. Because the characters are not yet known by us, I've showed them at a distance and little more than silhouettes. But there's a feeling of calm safety and lightheartedness.

In the second picture we get to know the boy a bit better. We're closer in on him. We have a sense of his spirit and gaiety; he's acting out his favorite dream in a friendly surrounding. But in the third picture we see his harsh awakening. The heads are large; we're close in; what they're looking at is important and is affecting the boy deeply. He realizes for the first time that his beloved sport can have a cruel aspect, and it's implicit that the world he's known until now is gone forever.

I've deliberately avoided the redundancy of precisely echoing the text; Trezor is not shown chasing the bird or bringing it back in his jaws. I think that where the words are powerful, as they are here, it weakens the effect to simplemindedly match the pictures to them. Much better to have the retrieval imagined; and this is especially true of the injured bird itself. The father and son look down, and we know they see the dying bird in their hands. I've left it to their attitudes, the sobriety of their expressions, the wincing shoulder of the boy, to convey their reactions.

In the fourth picture I've tried to suggest the effect on the boy of this first encounter with raw life. His back is toward us now. The attitude of his body is no longer carefree. He even droops a bit as he walks slowly away. The landscape is suddenly harsh, and, for the first time, there's a fence in it.

Merle Shore

The Quail

A story by Ivan Turgenev,
with pictures by Merle Shore

*Once in a while a person remembers
some childhood experience and writes it so vividly
that the reader lives the experience with him.
This is such a story.
It is a story with complicated sentences and many difficult words,
but by arranging the sentences into small chunks of meaning,
we have made it possible for you to read language
that perhaps you didn't know you could read.*

I was ten
when what I am going
to tell you now
happened to me.

It was summer.
I lived at the time
with my father
on a farm
in the south of Russia.
The farm was surrounded
by several miles of steppe.[1]
The flat steppe was cut
here and there
by shallow ravines,
overgrown with bushes
and stretching away
in the distance
like long, green serpents.
Little streams trickled
at the bottom
of these ravines.

[1] flat plains common to Russia

Little paths led to the water,
and in the damp mud
trails of birds
and small animals
crisscrossed each other.
They needed good water
as much as people.
My father was
a passionate[2] sportsman;
and as soon
as he got a free moment
and the weather was fine,
he would take his shotgun,
put his hunting bag
over his shoulder,
call his old dog Trezor,
and go off
to shoot partridges and quail.
Near the ravines
one often found
little circular holes
in the dry dust,
the places
where the partridges
were cleaning themselves.

[2] intense, keen, strong

99

Old Trezor
would immediately point,
his tail trembling
and the skin furrowing[3]
on his forehead,
while my father turned pale
and cautiously cocked his gun.
He often took me with him. . . .
And I did enjoy it tremendously!
I shoved my trousers
into my boot tops,
put a flask of water
over my shoulder
and imagined
myself a sportsman!
I was dripping with sweat,
small pebbles got
into my boots,
but I did not feel any fatigue
and did not lag
behind my father.
And when I heard a shot
and saw a bird fall,

[3] wrinkling

I skipped about
and even yelled—
I was so happy!
What would I not have given
to be able to fire a gun myself
and kill partridges and quail!
But my father told me
that I would not have a gun
before I was twelve;
and even then he would give me
only a one-barreled gun
and would let me fire
only at larks.
We had thousands of larks
near our farm;
on a nice, sunny day
hundreds of them flew
weaving in the clear sky,
rising higher and higher
and ringing like little bells.
I looked upon them
as my future booty
and took aim at them
with a stick which I carried
over my shoulder instead of a gun.

It is very easy to hit them
when they hover about
four or six feet
above the ground,
    quivering,
before suddenly diving
into the grass.

One day
Father and I went shooting—
it was on the eve
of St. Peter's Day.
At that time,
at the beginning of July,
young partridges
are still too small,
and Father did not want
to shoot them.

He went to the small oak bushes
growing near a field of rye
where there were always quail
to be had.
Suddenly Trezor pointed;
my father shouted, "Take it!"
and a quail leapt out
from under Trezor's very nose—
and flew away.
Only she flew away
in a very peculiar way:
she turned somersaults,
twisted around in the air,
fell on the ground,
just as though
she had been wounded
or had a broken wing.
Trezor rushed after her
as fast as he could
which he did not usually do
when a bird flew properly.
My father could not even fire,
for he was afraid
of hitting the dog.
All of a sudden
I saw Trezor leap forward
and catch the quail.
He caught her
and brought her to my father.
My father took her and put her
on the palm of his hand.
I ran up.

"What was the matter?" I asked.
"Was she wounded?"

"No," replied my father,
"she was not wounded.
I expect she must have a nest
with little chicks
somewhere near here,
and she deliberately pretended
to be wounded
so that the dog might think
he could catch her easily."

"Why did she do that?" I asked.

"Why," replied my father,
"to lead the dog away
from her chicks.
She would have flown properly
  afterward.
Only this time
she made a mistake.
She pretended a little too well
and Trezor caught her."

"So she isn't wounded?"
I asked again.

"No, of course not,
but I don't think
she's going to live.
Trezor must have crushed her
between his teeth."

I moved closer to the quail.
She lay motionless
on my father's hand
with her little head
hanging down.

She looked at me sideways
with one of her small
    brown eyes.
And suddenly
I felt so sorry for her!

"Daddy," I said,
"perhaps she won't die..."
And I wanted to stroke
the quail on the head.

But my father said to me,
"No! Watch.
In a moment
her legs will stretch out,
she will tremble all over,
and her eyes will close."
And so it happened.
When her eyes were closed,
I burst out crying.

"What's the matter?"
my father asked.

"I'm sorry for her," I said.
"She was only doing her duty,
and she was killed!"

"She was trying
to be a little too clever,"
my father said.
"Only Trezor was cleverer
than she."

My father was about
to put the quail
into his hunting bag,
but I begged him
to give her to me.
I held her carefully
in both my hands,
breathed on her—
but she did not stir.

"You're wasting your time,
    old fellow," my father said.
"You won't bring her back to life.
    You see how
    her head is drooping."
I raised her head gently
    by the beak,
    but as soon
    as I took away my hand,
    it fell down again.
"Who is going to feed
    her little ones?" I asked.

My father looked intently at me.
"Don't worry," he said,
"the cock-quail, their father,
    will feed them.
    Wait a moment," he added.
"Isn't Trezor pointing again?
    I wonder if it's the nest.
    Yes, so it is."

And so it was.
Two paces from Trezor's face,
four little chicks lay snugly,
close together in the grass.

They were clinging
to one another,
stretching out their necks
and breathing ever so quickly
and all together,
just as though
they were quivering!
They were already covered
with feathers;
there was no sign
of any down on them;
only their little tails
were still short.
"Daddy, Daddy," I shouted
    at the top of my voice,
"call Trezor off,
    or he'll kill them too!"

My father called Trezor back
and sat down under a bush
a little further away
to have his lunch.
But I remained near the nest.

Five days later
my father and I came again
to that same place.
The nest was empty.
There was not a trace
of the little birds.
My father assured me
that the cock-quail
must have taken them away,
and when,
a few paces from that spot,
an old cock-quail
suddenly flew out of a bush,
my father did not fire at him...
And I thought:
"My father is a kind man!"

The surprising thing
about it is this:
from that day
my passion for hunting
completely disappeared.
I no longer thought of the time
when my father
would make me a present
of a gun!

language works in chunks of meaning

When man invented
written language,
he immediately found the need
for additional inventions
to make that language work.
He, therefore, invented
capital letters, periods,
commas, quotation marks,
paragraph indentions,
and other signals
to help the reader *hear*
what he was *saying.*
The success of written language
is its resemblance
to oral language.
I am sure
all of you are accustomed
to pausing or hesitating
whenever you encounter a comma
or a period in a sentence.
This is one of the ways
that the writer shows you
how he groups the words
and how the sentence sounds.
Now I am suggesting
that you learn
to group words you read
even when there is no punctuation
to guide you.
You'll be surprised
how quickly you can learn
to see as one chunk
certain words
that must hang together
if you are to unravel
the sentence meaning.
For example,
look at this sentence:

The wild bugle of the bull elk
is one of the most exciting sounds
in the animal kingdom.

This sentence is composed
of five chunks of meaning:

1) The wild bugle
2) of the bull elk
3) is one
4) of the most exciting sounds
5) in the animal kingdom.

To have paused
after the word *wild*
or after the word *bull*
in reading this sentence
would have destroyed
the meaning of the sentence.
A reader cannot group words
just "any old way."
He must figure out
which words chunk together
to form meaning.
Unfortunately,
when children learn to read,
so much attention is paid
to individual words
that few of them ever learn
to see and to read words
in natural groupings.
I have known children
who stop dead still
in the middle of a sentence,
refusing to go on
until they can "figure out"
the unknown word.
If they would just keep going,
they would often find
that the chunk of meaning itself
or the complete sentence
reveals the meaning
of the unknown word.

For example, the word *bugle*
in the first chunk of meaning
of the sample sentence
finally reveals itself
(if you aren't familiar
with this name for an elk's call)
in the second
and fifth chunks of meaning.
A good reader learns to believe
that unknown words
will become known
as he reads further
into a sentence or a paragraph.
In this book
we have done a special thing
to help you work your way
through unknown words
and difficult sentences.
Many of the stories
are printed in a style
that reveals the chunks of meaning
in each sentence.
As you get the habit
of viewing every sentence this way,
you learn to find
the chunks of meaning
even though the sentence
is printed in unbroken lines.
And now for a slow-motion picture
of how a sentence works:

An essay by Bill Martin, Jr.

The memory of the first chunk
of meaning is stored in
your mind as you move
from it to the
second and
third.

Mother didn't seem too surprised and neither did Grampa

Language
works in chunks
of meaning. The first
chunk interlocks with the
second, with the third, and so on,
to the end of the sentence.

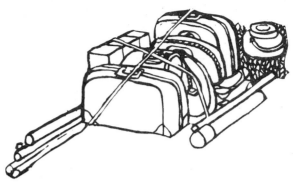

that, just as we gathered in the backyard with our gear,

Each chunk has its own meaning,
but it also becomes part of
a larger meaning that is
developing as you
read farther
into the
sentence.

Vacation Blues

An Excursion into the Time and Space
of a Sentence

By Bill Martin, Jr.,
with drawings by Leo and Diane Dillon

Hooper goofed, this time but good!, falling right into Dad

The sentence began on the last
page. It will continue
onto the next page.
So the sentence
is moving
through
space.

It
now has
been several
seconds since you
started reading this
sentence. So the sentence
is actually moving through time.

and causing him to have an explosion at the very time

As
you read
to the end of the
sentence, you, too, have
moved through time and space.
Reading is like riding in a car.
You move from one chunk of meaning to
another to arrive at a new destination.

we were finishing our packing to leave on our vacation.

With this last chunk of meaning, the
sentence itself becomes complete.
All of the chunks now form
into a larger and some-
what new meaning.
And you're ready
to move into
the next
sentence.

113

The Two Frogs

Once upon a time in the country of Japan there lived two frogs, one of whom made his home in a ditch near the town of Osaka, on the sea coast, while the other dwelt in a clear little stream which ran through the city of Kyoto. At such a great distance apart, they had never even heard of each other; but, funnily enough, the idea came into both their heads at once that they should like to see a little of the world, and the frog who lived at Kyoto wanted to visit Osaka, and the frog who lived at Osaka wished to go to Kyoto, where the great Mikado had his palace.

So one fine morning in the spring, they both set out along the road that led from Kyoto to Osaka, one from one end and the other from the other.

The journey was more tiring than they expected, for they did not know much about traveling, and halfway between the two towns there rose a mountain which had to be climbed. It took them a long time and a great many hops to reach the top, but there they were at last, and what was the surprise of each to see another frog before him! They looked at each other for a moment without speaking, and then fell into conversation, and explained the cause of their meeting so far from their homes. It was delightful to find that they both felt the same wish—to learn a little more of their native country—and as there was no sort of hurry they stretched themselves out in a cool, damp place and agreed that they would have a good rest before they parted to go their ways.

"What a pity we are not bigger," said the Osaka frog, "and then we could see both towns from here and tell if it is worth our while going on."

"Oh, that is easily managed," returned the Kyoto frog. "We have only got to stand up on our hind legs, and hold on to each other, and then we can each look at the town he is traveling to."

This idea pleased the Osaka frog so much that he at once jumped up and put his front paws on the shoulder of his friend, who had risen also. There they both stood, stretching themselves as high as they could, and holding each other tightly, so that they might not fall down. The Kyoto frog turned his nose towards Osaka, and the Osaka frog turned his nose towards Kyoto; but the foolish things forgot that when they stood up, their great eyes lay in the backs of their heads, and that though their noses might point to the places to which they wanted to go, their eyes beheld the places from which they had come.

"Dear me!" cried the Osaka frog; "Kyoto is exactly like Osaka. It is certainly not worth such a long journey. I shall go home."

"If I had had any idea that Osaka was only a copy of Kyoto I should never have traveled all this way," exclaimed the frog from Kyoto, and as he spoke, he took his hands from his friend's shoulders and they both fell down on the grass.

Then they took a polite farewell of each other and set off for home again, and to the end of their lives, they believed that Osaka and Kyoto, which are so different to look at as two towns can be, were as like as two peas.

An old Japanese folktale, retold by Marie Shedlock

LONE DOG

I'm a lean dog, a keen dog,
    a wild dog, and lone;
I'm a rough dog, a tough dog,
    hunting on my own;
I'm a bad dog, a mad dog,
    teasing silly sheep;
I love to sit and bay the moon,
    to keep fat souls from sleep.

I'll never be a lap dog,
    licking dirty feet,
A sleek dog, a meek dog,
    cringing for my meat,
Not for me the fireside,
    the well-filled plate,
But shut door, and sharp stone,
    and cuff and kick and hate.

Not for me the other dogs,
    running by my side,
Some have run a short while,
    but none of them would bide,
Oh, mine is still the lone trail,
    the hard trail, the best,
Wide wind, and wild stars,
    and hunger of the quest!

A poem by Irene Rutherford McLeod,
picture by Terri Payor

using your ears in reading

We are so accustomed to thinking of reading
as being done by the eye,
that we forget that reading began for each of us
as we learned to hear the familiar sounds of our language.
For example, until these words are anchored in your ear,
your eye really isn't much good in telling you
how to pronounce words like *amen, weigh, ought, laughter.*

Ask yourself as you read this poem
whether it is your eye or your ear that manages the strange words:

ONE, TWO, THREE—GOUGH!

Boys: To make some bread you must have dough,
Girls: Isn't that sough?

Boys: If the sky is clear all through,
Is the color of it blough?

Girls: When is the time to put your hand to the plough?
Boys: Nough!

Girls: The handle on the pump near the trough
Nearly fell ough.

Boys: Bullies sound rough and tough enough,
But you can often call their blough.

by Eve Merriam

And here's a poem in which none of the words are difficult.
But again, the reading of the poem is largely the job of the ears.
Getting the rhythm and swing of the poem is a matter of hearing it.
The more you hear it spoken, the better your eye can read it.

THE HAG

The Hag is astride,
This night for to ride;
The Devil and she together;
Through thick and through thin,
Now out and then in,
Though ne'er so foul be the weather.

A thorn or a burr
She takes for a spur,
With a lash of a bramble she rides now;
Through brakes and through briars,
O'er ditches and mires,
She follows the Spirit that guides now.

No beast, for his food
Dares now range the wood,
But hushed in his lair he lies lurking;
While mischiefs, by these,
On land and on seas,
At noon of night are a-working.

The storm will arise
And trouble the skies;
This night, and more for the wonder,
The ghost from the tomb
Affrighted shall come,
Called out by the clap of the thunder.

by Robert Herrick

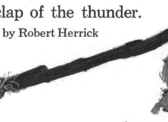

An essay by Bill Martin, Jr.,
illustration by Wayne Ensrud

119

The Birth and Growth of a Tree

Every seed on every tree carries within it the miniature of another tree-to-be. Formed on the branches during the summer, spread by animals or autumn winds, the seeds lie dormant—sleeping—during the winter. When the soil grows warm, when spring rains come, changes begin to take place within those seeds that have fallen in places favorable to growing. The cells within the tiny seed "awaken" and begin to grow. Soon each cell has grown so large that it divides itself into two cells, and later each of these two cells divides again, and on and on. And a process of growth begins that can perpetuate itself for centuries. This marvelous process gives the world its forests.

3 As soon as the tiny root tip penetrates the soil, the tree is not only fixed in the ground, but is capable of absorbing water and mineral nutriments.

2 The growing "tree-to-be" splits the shell of the seed. Responding to gravity — whichever way the seed lies — the root twines its way toward the ground.

1 The "tree-to-be" inside the seed — complete with tiny leaves, stem, and a point that will become a root — is bedded in a food supply that keeps it alive during the winter.

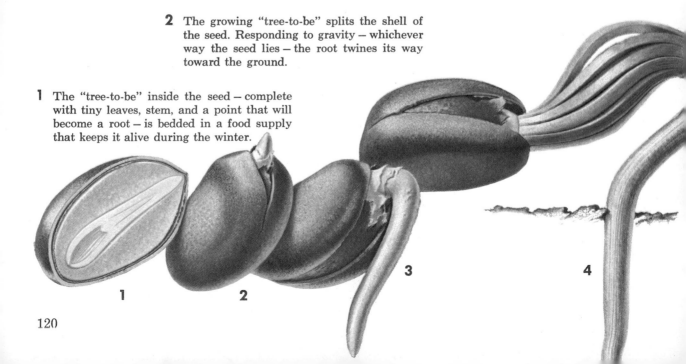

1   2   3   4

6 Hidden at the base of the leaves is the "terminal bud." Within this cluster of actively dividing cells, all upward growth takes place.

4,5 The leaves of the tree-to-be emerge from the shell and create a supply of chlorophyll. Now the tree can manufacture its own food from water in the soil and carbon dioxide in the air.

Based on materials provided by

ST REGIS

121

This tree is 62 years old. It's been through fire and drought, plague and plenty. And all of this is recorded in its rings.

Each spring and summer a tree adds new layers of wood to its trunk. The wood formed in spring grows fast and is lighter because it consists of large cells. In summer, growth is slower; the wood has smaller cells and is darker. So when the tree is cut, the layers appear as alternating rings of light and dark wood.

Count the dark rings, and you know the tree's age. Study the rings, and you can learn much more. Many things affect the way the tree grows and thus alter the shape, thickness, color and evenness of the rings.

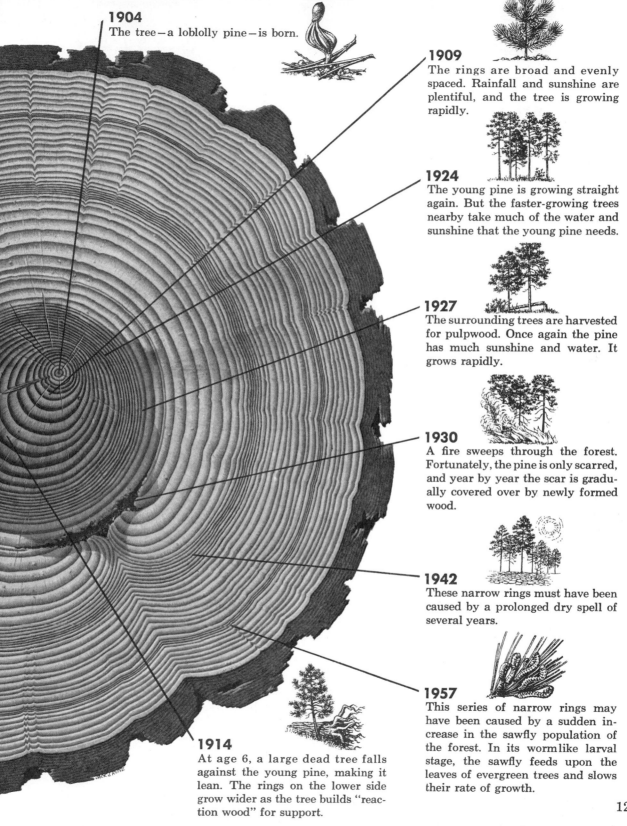

1904
The tree—a loblolly pine—is born.

1909
The rings are broad and evenly spaced. Rainfall and sunshine are plentiful, and the tree is growing rapidly.

1924
The young pine is growing straight again. But the faster-growing trees nearby take much of the water and sunshine that the young pine needs.

1927
The surrounding trees are harvested for pulpwood. Once again the pine has much sunshine and water. It grows rapidly.

1930
A fire sweeps through the forest. Fortunately, the pine is only scarred, and year by year the scar is gradually covered over by newly formed wood.

1942
These narrow rings must have been caused by a prolonged dry spell of several years.

1957
This series of narrow rings may have been caused by a sudden increase in the sawfly population of the forest. In its wormlike larval stage, the sawfly feeds upon the leaves of evergreen trees and slows their rate of growth.

1914
At age 6, a large dead tree falls against the young pine, making it lean. The rings on the lower side grow wider as the tree builds "reaction wood" for support.

123

No longer is any part of a log wasted in lumbering. Even the wood scraps are used for making pulp.

Did you ever wonder where all the different size boards used in building a house come from? Did you ever wonder what happens to the rest of the tree once the main part of a log has been sawed into lumber? By careful reading of this picture, you will find the answer to many of the questions you might have about the logging industry. And you

also might find that your unanswered questions will send you to the library or other sources for additional information. At one time, up to 50 per cent of some logs cut into lumber went unused. Today, sawmills know how to get the most from every log — even the scraps and chips which are turned into pulp for making paper.

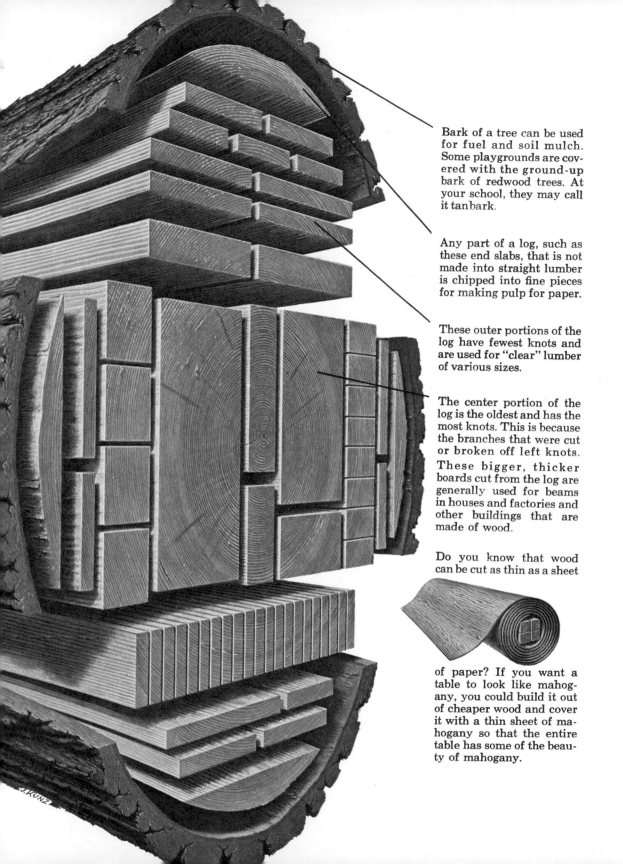

Bark of a tree can be used for fuel and soil mulch. Some playgrounds are covered with the ground-up bark of redwood trees. At your school, they may call it tanbark.

Any part of a log, such as these end slabs, that is not made into straight lumber is chipped into fine pieces for making pulp for paper.

These outer portions of the log have fewest knots and are used for "clear" lumber of various sizes.

The center portion of the log is the oldest and has the most knots. This is because the branches that were cut or broken off left knots. These bigger, thicker boards cut from the log are generally used for beams in houses and factories and other buildings that are made of wood.

Do you know that wood can be cut as thin as a sheet of paper? If you want a table to look like mahogany, you could build it out of cheaper wood and cover it with a thin sheet of mahogany so that the entire table has some of the beauty of mahogany.

OSCAR WILDE'S

The Selfish Giant

Illustration by Betty Fraser

Every afternoon, as they were coming from school, the children used to go and play in the Giant's garden.

It was a large lovely garden, with soft green grass. Here and there over the grass stood beautiful flowers like stars, and there were twelve peach trees that in the springtime broke out into delicate blossoms of pink and pearl.

In the autumn the peach trees bore rich fruit. The birds sat on the trees and sang so sweetly that the children used to stop their games in order to listen to them. "How happy we are here!" they cried to each other.

One day the Giant came back. He had been to visit his friend, the Cornish ogre, and had stayed with him for seven years. After the seven years were over, he had said all that he had to say, for his conversation was limited, and he determined to return to his own castle. When he arrived, he saw the children playing in the garden.

"What are you doing there?" he cried in a very gruff voice, and the children ran away.

"My own garden is my own garden," said the Giant; "anyone can understand that, and I will allow nobody to play in it but myself." So he built a high wall all around it, and put up a notice-board.

TRESPASSERS
WILL BE
PROSECUTED

He was a very selfish Giant. The poor children now had nowhere to play. They tried to play on the road, but the road

was very dusty and full of hard stones, and they did not like it. They used to wander round the high wall when their lessons were over and talk about the beautiful garden inside. "How happy we were there," they said to each other.

Then the Spring came, and all over the country there were little blossoms and little birds. Only in the garden of the Selfish Giant it was still winter.

Birds did not care to sing in it as there were no children, and the trees forgot to blossom. Once a beautiful flower put its head out from the grass, but when it saw the notice-board, it was so sorry for the children that it slipped back into the ground again and went to sleep.

The only people who were pleased were the Snow and the Frost. "Spring has forgotten this garden," they cried, "so we will live here all the year round." The Snow covered up the grass with his great white cloak, and the Frost painted all the trees silver. Then they invited the North Wind to stay with them, and he came.

He was wrapped in furs, and he roared all day about the garden and blew the chimney-pots down. "This is a delightful spot," he said; "we must ask the Hail on a visit."

So the Hail came. Every day for three hours he rattled on the roof of the castle till he broke most of the slates, and then he ran round and round the garden as fast as he could go. He was dressed in gray, and his breath was like ice.

"I cannot understand why the Spring is so late in coming," said the Selfish Giant, as he sat at the window and looked out at his cold white garden; "I hope there will be a change in the weather."

But the Spring never came nor the Summer. The Autumn gave golden fruit to every garden, but to the Giant's garden she gave none. "He is too selfish," she said. So it was always winter there, and the North Wind and the Hail and the Frost and the Snow danced about through the trees.

One morning the Giant was lying awake in bed when he heard some lovely music. It sounded so sweet to his ears that he thought it must be the King's musicians passing by. It was really only a little linnet singing outside his window, but it was so long since he had heard a bird sing in his garden that it seemed to him to be the most beautiful music in the world. Then the Hail stopped dancing over his head, and the North Wind ceased roaring, and a delicious perfume came to him through the open casement. "I believe the Spring has come at last," said the Giant; and he jumped out of bed and looked out.

What did he see?

He saw a most wonderful sight. Through a little hole in the wall the children had crept in, and they were sitting in the branches of the trees. In every tree that he could see there was a little child. And the trees were so glad to have the children back again that they had covered themselves with blossoms and were waving their arms gently above the children's heads. The birds were flying about and twittering with delight, and the flowers were looking up through the green grass and laughing.

It was a lovely scene, only in one corner it was still winter. It was the farthest corner of the garden, and in it was standing a little boy. He was so small that he could not reach up to the branches of the tree, and he was wandering all round it, crying bitterly. The poor tree was still quite covered with frost and snow, and the North Wind was blowing and roaring above it.

"Climb up! little boy," said the tree, and it bent its branches down as low as it could; but the boy was too tiny.

And the Giant's heart melted as he looked out. "How selfish I have been!" he said; "now I know why the Spring would not come here. I will put that poor little boy on the top of the tree, and then I will knock down the wall, and my garden shall be the children's playground for ever and ever." He was really sorry for what he had done.

So he crept downstairs and opened the front door quite softly and went out into the garden. But when the children saw him, they were so frightened that they all ran away, and the garden became winter again. Only the little boy did not run, for his eyes were so full of tears that he did not see the Giant coming.

And the Giant stole up behind him and took him gently in his hand and put him up into the tree. And the tree broke at once into blossoms, and the birds came and sang on it, and the little boy stretched out his two arms and flung them round the Giant's neck and kissed him. And the other children, when

they saw that the Giant was not wicked any longer, came running back, and with them came the Spring.

"It is your garden now, little children," said the Giant, and he took a great axe and knocked down the wall. And when the people were going to market at twelve o'clock, they found the Giant playing with the children in the most beautiful garden they had ever seen.

All day long they played, and in the evening they came to the Giant to bid him good-by.

"But where is your little companion?" he said. "The boy I put into the tree." The Giant loved him the best because he had kissed him.

"We don't know," answered the children; "he has gone away."

"You must tell him to be sure and come here tomorrow," said the Giant. But the children said that they did not know where he lived and had never seen him before; and the Giant felt very sad.

Every afternoon, when school was over, the children came and played with the Giant. But the little boy whom the Giant loved was never seen again. The Giant was very kind to all the children, yet he longed for his first little friend and often spoke of him. "How I would like to see him!" he used to say.

Years went over, and the Giant grew very old and feeble. He could not play about any more, so he sat in a huge armchair and watched the children at their games and admired his garden. "I have many beautiful flowers," he said; "but the children are the most beautiful flowers of all."

One winter morning he looked out of his window as he was dressing. He did not hate the Winter now for he knew that it was merely the Spring asleep, and that the flowers were resting.

Suddenly he rubbed his eyes in wonder, and looked and looked. It certainly was a marvelous sight. In the farthest corner of the garden was a tree quite covered with lovely white blossoms. Its branches were all golden, and silver fruit hung down from them, and underneath it stood the little boy he had loved.

Downstairs ran the Giant in great joy and out into the garden. He hastened across the grass and came near to the child. And when he came quite close his face grew red with anger, and he said, "Who hath dared to wound thee?" For on the palms of the child's hands were prints of two nails, and the prints of two nails were on the little feet.

"Who hath dared to wound thee?" cried the Giant; "tell me, that I may take my sword and slay him." "Nay!" answered the child; "but these are the wounds of Love." "Who are thou?" said the Giant, and a strange awe fell on him, and he knelt before the little child.

And the child smiled on the Giant, and said to him, "You let me play once in your garden; today you shall come with me to my garden, which is Paradise."

And when the children ran in
that afternoon, they found the
Giant lying dead under the tree,
all covered with white blossoms.

using your eyes to hear

An essay by Bill Martin, Jr.

Picture reading is an important way
that we use our eyes in reading.
With the advent[1] of television,
outdoor advertising, picture books,
and magazines that tell stories
largely by pictures,
picture reading has become
more and more a part of our lives.
Picture reading takes time
    and thought.
It is more than just looking at
or naming the objects in a picture.

It is studying the picture
to see how the objects
affect one another
and how the picture affects you.
A thoughtful picture
may cause you to ponder
or to do further research
or to write a story or a poem
or to organize
odd bits of information
that you have never
really brought together.

[1] coming

Some of the best reading occurs
when you have the chance
to read both pictures and words.
In fact, the sudden increase
in the number of fine books
with related text and pictures
shows how appealing
"picture-story" books can be.
Don't make the mistake
of thinking that picture stories
are not meant for you.
One of the most challenging stories
in this very book
is a picture story.
You may be surprised to find
that the drawings take as much,
or more, space than the print,
but once you have begun
the adventures of *Old Stormalong*,
you'll discover that you learn much
about his character
by studying the pictures.
And, incidentally, all
of the *Sounds of Language* books
have been designed
to make picture reading one
of your important reading skills.

0 MPH	10 MPH	20 MPH	30 MPH	40 MPH	50 MPH	60 MPH

bee   common bat   brown pelican   herring gull   dragonfly
blue jay   great horned owl   starling   wild turkey   crow   Canada goose
               canvasback
African elephant   giraffe   ostrich
tortoise   mole   sheep   racing camel   man   bison   emu   horse   gnu
      mouse   greyhound   Mongolian gazelle
       black mamba   wart hog   hare   cheetah
black racer   roadrunner
         weasel   cat   red fox
                    trout   sailfish
beaver   dolphin
    polar bear
     loon   gentoo penguin   flying fish
     man   green turtle   tarpon
shrimp   eel   otter   finback whale   tuna

The Top Speeds of Animals

If mammals were pitted against insects, fishes, reptiles and birds in a race, they would fare like this: The cheetah, running at a top speed of 70 miles an hour, would be out in front, outdistanced only by the golden eagle, Indian swift and peregrine falcon. But having less staying power, the cheetah would eventually be overtaken by the Mongolian gazelle, whose short body and long legs give it great endurance on long runs.

On the bottom of the painting is a scale of speeds in miles per hour. Man is shown in sprints—the 100-yard dash and the 100-yard swim. The race horse is mounted because a horse will run faster if goaded by a rider.

80 MPH   **90 MPH**   **100 MPH**

golden eagle   peregrine falcon
Indian swift

AIR

LAND

WATER

Illustration by Rudolph Freund from *The Mammals* © 1963 Time Inc.

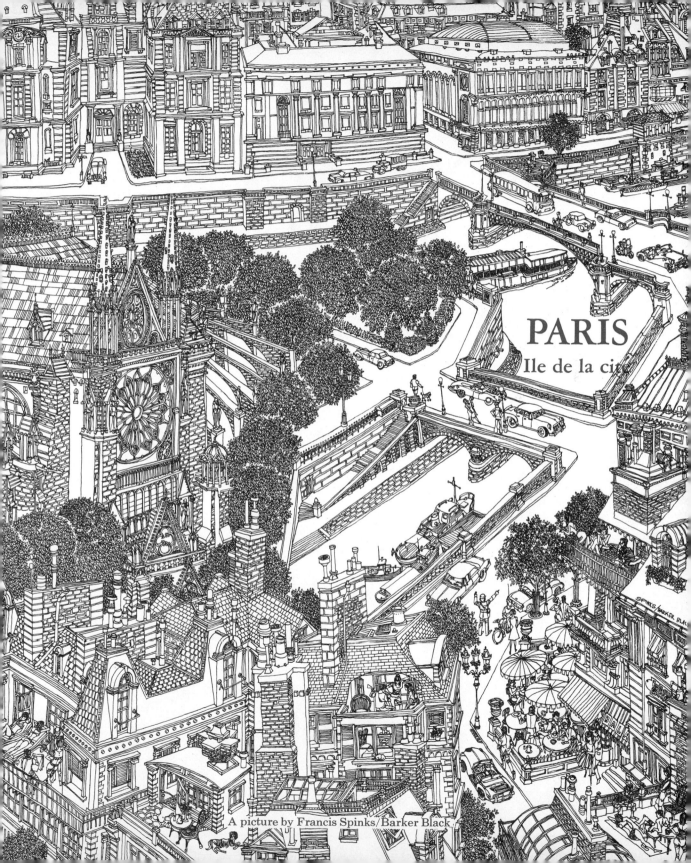

PARIS

Ile de la cité

A picture by Francis Spinks/Barker Black

Time Line into Space

A graph of space explorations

About 1232 A.D.   Chinese invent rockets.

About 1500   *Wahn Hoo:* a Chinese emperor lost his life in man's first attempted rocket flight. Forty-seven rockets were attached to his chair and ignited.

About 1800   Long-range military rockets developed in England by Sir William Congreve.

1812   Congreve's rockets used by English against Americans during siege of Ft. McHenry.

[1] *rocket:* a space vehicle supplied with fuel that combusts to project the vehicle into (or through) the air

1926   First liquid-fueled rocket[1] developed by Robert H. Goddard, U.S.A.

1930   Goddard fires rocket that attains altitude of 2,000 feet and speed of 500 miles per hour.

[3]*orbit:* path around the earth or other solar body

[2]*satellite:* Up to the last decade, this term was used to mean a moon circling a planet. Now it has come also to mean a man-made body (artificial satellite) in orbit around the earth or other solar body.

11-3-57   *Sputnik II:* carries a dog into orbit around earth, U.S.S.R.

10-4-57   *Sputnik I:* first man-made satellite[2] to orbit[3] the earth, U.S.S.R.

2-4-49   *Two-Stage Rocket:* first object hurled beyond earth's atmosphere, U.S.A.

12-14-46   *V-2 Rocket:* captured from Germans and first fired by U.S.A., reaches altitude of 114 miles.

1940-45   Germans develop long-range rocket used to bombard London during World War II.

1–31–58   *Explorer I:* first U.S. satellite
to orbit earth.

3–17–58   *Vanguard I:* second U.S.
satellite to orbit earth.

5–15–58   *Sputnik III:* Russia's third
satellite to orbit.

10–11–58   *Pioneer I:* first attempt to
reach the moon, U.S.A.

12–18–58   *Atlas:* first communications
satellite.[4] President
Eisenhower's Christmas
greetings are transmitted to
Europe by way of a satellite,
U.S.A.

[4] *communications satellite:* a satellite
equipped to receive signals (such as
television waves) from one spot on earth
and transmit those signals to another
part of the earth

1–2–59   *Luna I:* first man-made
satellite to orbit the sun,
U.S.S.R.

[8] *instrument capsule:* a container of instruments sent up into space to collect information which will be studied when the container re-enters the earth's atmosphere and is retrieved

[7] *weather satellite:* a satellite equipped with instruments that collect information about the weather and transmit that information back to earth

[6] *spacecraft:* any device, either manned or unmanned, placed in orbit about the earth or in a trajectory to another planet

8–10–60 *Discoverer XIII:* first retrieval of instrument capsule[8] from outer space, U.S.A.

5–15–60 *Space Ship I:* first spacecraft to orbit earth with dummy spaceman, U.S.S.R.

4–1–60 *Tiros I:* first weather satellite,[7] U.S.A.

10–4–59 *Luna III:* first space vehicle to fly around the moon. Sends back photographs of the side of the moon never before seen by man, U.S.S.R.

9–12–59 *Luna II:* first spacecraft[6] to hit the moon, U.S.S.R.

8–7–59 *Explorer VI:* first satellite to take television photographs of earth and transmit them back to earth, U.S.A.

5–28–59 *Jupiter Nose Cone:* two monkeys ride 300 miles into space on suborbital[5] flight, U.S.A.

[5] *suborbital:* any flight of an object thrust into space that does not go into orbit

3–3–59 *Pioneer IV:* second planetoid to orbit sun, U.S.A.

8-19-60

Space Ship II: two dogs sent into orbit and returned safely to earth, U.S.S.R.

11-12-60

Discoverer XVII: second instrument capsule retrieved from space, this one caught in midair by airplane, U.S.A.

2-4-61

Sputnik V: heaviest satellite yet launched, 14,292 pounds, U.S.S.R.

2-12-61

Venus Rocket I: first rocket launched from an orbiting satellite, heads toward Venus, U.S.S.R.

2-22-61

Véronique Rocket: first suborbital vehicle launched by France. Carries live rat 90 miles.

4-12-61

Vostok I: first man into space. Astronaut Gagarin orbits earth once in 108 minutes and returns safely, U.S.S.R.

5-5-61

Freedom 7: second man into space. Astronaut Shepard makes 15-minute suborbital flight, U.S.A.

7-21-61

Liberty Bell 7: Astronaut Grissom makes 16-minute suborbital flight, U.S.A.

8-6-61

Vostok II: second man to orbit earth. Astronaut Titov, 17 orbits in 25 hours, U.S.S.R.

2-20-62

Friendship 7: first American into orbit. Astronaut Glenn makes 3 orbits in 4 hours 56 minutes, traveling 81,000 miles.

4-24-62

Ranger IV: second space vehicle to crash-land[9] on moon, U.S.A.

4-26-62

Ariel I: first international space vehicle launched, England-U.S.A.

5-24-62

Aurora 7: Astronaut Carpenter makes 3 orbits, U.S.A.

7-10-62

Telstar I: communications satellite, first to transmit television broadcasts across Atlantic, U.S.A.

8-11-62

Vostok III: Astronaut Nikolayev orbits earth 64 times, 1,625,000 miles, 92 hours. First live television broadcast from a space ship, U.S.S.R.

[9] *crash landing:* the landing of a space vehicle, on a satellite or planet, with such force that it destroys the workings of the spacecraft

8–12–62

Vostok IV: Astronaut Popovich attempts rendezvous[10] in space with Astronaut Nikolayev in *Vostok III.* They missed by only 4 or 5 miles, U.S.S.R.

8–27–62

Mariner II: successfully launched toward Venus, U.S.A.

9–27–62

Alouette I: second international space vehicle, Canada-U.S.A.

10–3–62

Sigma 7: Astronaut Schirra, 6 orbits, U.S.A.

12–14–62

Mariner II: (launched 8–27–62) passes within 21,000 miles of Venus and radios data 36 million miles back to earth, U.S.A.

5–15–63

Faith 7: Astronaut Cooper, 22 orbits, 34 hours 20 minutes, U.S.A.

6–14–63

Vostok V: Astronaut Bykovsky, 81 orbits in 4 days, 23 hours 6 minutes, U.S.S.R.

[10]*rendezvous:* A rendezvous would be involved, for example, traveling from the earth to dock at a space station.

6–16–63

Vostok VI: Astronaut Tereshkova, first woman into space. Orbits 3 days and passes within 3 miles of *Vostok V* in Russia's second attempt to rendezvous two vehicles in outer space.

1–30–64

Ranger VI: crash-lands on moon, U.S.A.

3–25–64

Italian Capsule: Italy's first suborbital spacecraft, launched by U.S. rocket.

3–27–64

Ariel II: second British satellite, orbited by U.S. rocket.

7–28–64

Ranger VII: sends back 4,000 photographs of moon's surface before crash-landing on moon, U.S.A.

10–12–64

Voskhod I: first space vehicle to carry three astronauts. Orbited 16 times in 24 hours, U.S.S.R.

11–28–64

Mariner IV: launched toward Mars, U.S.A.

11–30–64

Zond II: launched toward Mars, U.S.S.R.

12–15–64

San Marco: first Italian satellite, orbited by U.S. rocket.

3-18-65

Voskhod II: Astronaut Leonov leaves space capsule for man's first "walk" in space,[11] U.S.S.R.

3-21-65

Ranger IX: First television pictures of moon's surface. Space vehicle crash-lands on target, U.S.A.

3-23-65

Gemini III: Astronauts Grissom and Young make first use of spacecraft's rockets to change its flight pattern, U.S.A.

4-6-65

Early Bird: first communication satellite for commercial use, launched by American Telephone and Telegraph Company with help of U.S. government.

6-3-65

Gemini IV: Astronaut White becomes second man to walk in space, U.S.A.

6-8-65

Luna VII: a spacecraft launched from orbiting satellite, crash-lands on moon, U.S.S.R.

7-15-65

Mariner IV: (launched 11-28-64) passes within 6,118 miles of Mars and transmits first photographs of Mars 54 million miles back to earth, U.S.A.

7-16-65

Proton I: 26,000 pounds, heaviest satellite yet launched, U.S.S.R.

8-21-65

Gemini V: 8-day orbit, Astronauts Cooper and Conrad, U.S.A.

11-26-65

Asterix I: France's first satellite into orbit.

11-28-65

Alouette II: Canada's second satellite, launched from Cape Kennedy.

12-5-65

Gemini VII: Astronauts Borman and Lovell set record of 14 days in space, 206 orbits, over 5 million miles, U.S.A.

12-6-65

Fria I: France's second satellite, launched with U.S. rocket.

12-15-65

Gemini VI: Astronauts Schirra and Stafford blast into orbit and rendezvous with *Gemini VII* for first meeting of two spacecrafts in flight, U.S.A.

[11] *space walk:* The weightlessness of an object in space makes it possible for a man to "step outside" his space capsule and "walk about." His capsule does not move away from him because he and the capsule are traveling at the same rate of speed.

1-5-66

Mariner IV: (launched 11-28-64) still in orbit, 216 million miles from earth, still transmitting signals back to U.S.A.

1-31-66

Luna IX: first spacecraft to make soft landing[12] on moon and send back photographs, U.S.S.R.

2-22-66

Cosmos 110: two dogs orbited at an altitude higher than any living creature has yet flown, 22 days, U.S.S.R.

3-1-66

Venus Probe: spacecraft crash-lands into Venus. First spacecraft to make physical contact with another planet, U.S.S.R.

3-16-66

Gemini VIII: Astronauts Scott and Armstrong rendezvous with target vehicle. First docking[13] and undocking of two vehicles in space, U.S.A.

[12] *soft landing:* landing a space vehicle, on a satellite or planet, without damaging its instruments that are to collect information and transmit it back to earth

[13] *docking:* the joining together of two spacecraft; the meeting and hooking together of two spacecraft traveling in the same orbit

5-15-66

Nimbus II: largest weather satellite yet launched, U.S.A.

5-23-66

Europa I: first satellite launched by European Launcher Development Program, a cooperative venture by ten European nations.

5-30-66

Surveyor I: first American spacecraft to soft-land on moon. Sends back 11,150 photographs of moon's surface.

6-3-66

Gemini IX: Astronaut Cernan makes record space walk of 2 hours 9 minutes, U.S.A.

7-5-66

Apollo Project: 29-ton unmanned satellite, heaviest ever put into orbit, U.S.A.

7-18-66

Gemini X: Astronauts Young and Collins launch first satellite from manned spacecraft, U.S.A.

8-10-66

Lunar Orbiter I: America's first moon satellite.

9-12-66

Gemini XI: new altitude record of 850 miles by Astronauts Conrad and Gordon, U.S.A.

11-11-66

Gemini XII: Astronaut Aldrin sets new record, 2 hours 22 minutes, for time spent outside space capsule, U.S.A.

149

MEAT, MATÉ and MUSIC

THERE is no meal simpler to prepare than a gaucho dinner. Provided that you have a little fire built in the open field, then you need only two things— a big hunk of meat and a solid iron spike. That's all.

The gaucho seldom eats vegetables. He does not cultivate them, and, though they may be pretty to look at, vegetables to him are—chicken feed!

Occasionally, when the fancy takes him, he may prepare a potful of *puchero*. This puchero is second cousin to an Irish stew, or a Hungarian *gulyas*.

A story by Francis Kalnay, pictures by **Frank Aloise**

Like any good stew, the puchero is full of surprises. If you just dig in, a spoonful at a time, the thrill will remind you of a package party. You don't know what's coming next. Here a chunk of spicy sausage, there a slice of cabbage, then a piece of ham, next a carrot or a potato big as your fist.

Don't ever be afraid, when you are invited to partake of puchero, that you may not like it. You are bound to like some part of it. But if you flatly refuse to try it at all, then the fault is yours. There could be nothing wrong with the puchero prepared fresh on the pampas.

Your true gaucho is a meat-eater, if ever there were one. Meat! That's his business. He rides it, he herds it, and he eats it.

The gaucho needs no kitchen, no utensils, and no fancy service. Just let him pierce a big chunk of meat, say twenty pounds of beef, with an iron spit. He sticks

this into the ground at an angle above the fire. The rest is easy. He pokes the fire, turns the meat around, and pokes it with his knife, which is always sharp, as are his teeth.

If a juicy medium-done beefsteak is to your liking, sit down near the fire and help yourself. The gaucho loves company. And he loves to talk and to listen to stories, especially after the choicest cuts of the roast are gone.

He hasn't eaten too much, possibly only a couple of pounds, and if you say "*basta*—enough," he will throw the rest to the dogs.

Now is the time to place the kettle on the fire to have hot water for the *yerba maté*. He has his hollow gourd at hand and the ornamental silver tube with which he sips the bitter drink. You will find him somewhat impatient for his maté. When at last he has the taste of that famous Paraguayan beverage in his mouth, he settles back contented. If it's chilly, you will see him crouched near the fire, his poncho pulled close, happy just to watch the flames. And after a sip or two from the gourd, he'll turn to you and say, "Well, *amigo mio*, unless you have some interesting story to tell, I'll sing you a lovely song that Carmela taught me the other night. Let me just reach for my guitar. . . ." Any gaucho may tell you that.

But not Juan.

To begin with, Juan seldom went to the village dances and parties where one has a chance to meet new girls and hear new songs. He preferred to stay around camp, dance with the same girls, or sit in front of his fire late into the night and sing the oldtime gaucho songs. He had a lovely ringing voice, and sometimes, from a distance, it sounded mellow as the chimes of the chapel at the estancia. Although somewhat shy, he didn't mind singing in company when the gauchos around were his friends, but he was at his best when Pedrito was his only audience. Then he would lie on his back on the grass, facing the sky, and sing song after song as if he had one apiece for each little star. And once in a while he would sit up, and for no apparent reason, both he and Pedro would laugh out loud.

"That was a jolly old song, Pedrito. What do you say?"

The ponies, too, enjoyed the music. You would often find them grazing near the fire, and though you may not believe it, they really were listening.

Many evenings, when the stories had their turn, Chúcaro hardly stirred a step from his favorite spot near the fire. When Pedrito felt tired, he would climb on his pony's back, fold his arms around Chúcaro's neck, and cling there, listening to the story until his eyes closed. It might be that an outburst of laughter would wake him up, and, drowsy as he was, he would try to catch the drift of the story.

Then once more his hands would steal around the neck of Chúcaro, and he would whisper in the pony's ear, "You'll tell me the rest of the story tomorrow. Good night, my Chúcaro."

Then Juan would lift the boy from the pony, quietly lay him down on the broad seat of the cart, and cover him with a poncho.

The ability to sense the way a story or poem or article
has been put together is a valuable help
in getting more pleasure from the printed page.
Every good reader I know goes into a selection searching for clues
that would help him know what to expect as he reads further
into the selection.
    Let's look at an example:

A Man of Words

A man of words and not of deeds
Is like a garden full of weeds:
And when the weeds begin to grow,
It's like a garden full of snow;
And when the snow begins to fall,
It's like a bird upon the wall;

After reading the first six lines of this old rhyme,
you can make a hunch that every two lines are going to "feed into"
the next two lines in a rather simple but fascinating way.
Let's see if that is so:

____ ____ ____ [   ] away does fly,
____ ____ an eagle in the sky;
____ ____ ____ [   ] begins to roar,
____ ____ a lion at the door;
____ ____ ____ [   ] begins to crack,
____ ____ a stick across your back;
____ ____ ____ [   ] ____ ____ smart,
____ ____ a penknife in your heart;
____ ____ ____ [   ] ____ ____ bleed,
    You're dead, and dead, and dead indeed.

An old rhyme

Ah, now you can see how each new sentence is interlocked
with the last. Once you're sure that you see
how this interlocking is taking place,
you can read the rest of the rhyme
without having to look at every word.
All you need locate are the "cargo-bearing" words,
and your familiarity with the structure
lets you chant the rest of this rhyme
as if it were an old familiar "friend" you've known all your life.

Let's consider another example.
Do you recall at the beginning of the story "The Stone,"
on page 20, Tom is exuberant because he has enough fur pelts
from his fall trapping that he can buy his mother
an expensive Christmas gift?
At this point, you can guess something like this:

1. Aha! This story probably will revolve
   around the Christmas gift.
   Maybe Tom's gift won't arrive in time.
   Maybe his mother won't like it.
2. You can tell yourself,
   "I already know by the 'ring' of these first sentences
   and from the tenor of the pictures and the title
   that this is going to be a serious story.
   I also can tell that certain sentences
   and certain words may be a little difficult,
   so I'm going to proceed with 'my eyes and ears open'
   for clues that will make the reading easier."

Shortly thereafter in the story, Tom's furs are stolen
from his bicycle while he is chasing a pheasant.

3. "Oho!" you tell yourself. "Now I've got it.
   Tom's problem is to get the furs back
   so he can get the gift for his mother.
   This is what the story is all about."

But, suddenly, the story takes an unexpected turn.
Instead of Tom tearing off to find the thief,
he's remembering a lot of things
that happened to him earlier in the fall.

4. "I wonder why the author is letting the story backtrack?
   There must be a good reason! The author
   is going to tell me something important right now—
   something that will help me figure out in advance
   how Tom will get the Christmas gift for his mother."

The story now is dealing with the "good luck" stone
that Tom carries in his pocket.

5. "The author is telling us so much about the stone
   that it must be the key to solving Tom's problem.
   Moreover, the name of this story is *The Stone*.
   I've got it now! Tom is either going to give the stone
   to his mother, or he's going to trade it
   for something that he can use for a gift."

The story is still in the "flashback."
It tells more and more about Tom's trapping plans
and his love of the woods and the stream.

6. "I wonder why the author is giving us
   all this background on Tom?" you ask yourself.
   "I can't see that it has anything to do with the story.
   Rick is Tom's friend. He couldn't be the thief.
   Besides, most of this part of the story is about Tom,
   not Rick ...
   Oh, now I have it.
   The author is telling me all of this
   so I will know Tom well enough to *really* like him.
   The author is 'softening me up' to Tom
   so I'll get a real emotional wallop
   out of the ending of the story.
   The author certainly is putting this story together
   in a way that adds suspense to the finish.
   I wonder what happened to those furs?"

Tom goes to his friend, the jeweler.
He makes arrangements with Mr. Belden
to make the stone into a pendant
for his mother's Christmas gift.

7. "Now, I know why the author told me so much about Tom.
   He wants me to have deep sympathy and respect for Tom now
   as he gives up his 'good luck' piece."

It's Christmas morning.
The telephone rings! Tom's mother answers it.

8. "Ah! I knew it would happen.
   Here is the good news we've been waiting for.
   The furs have been found!"

Mr. Belden tells Tom's mother that the stone is valuable.
It will provide enough money for Tom's college education.

9. "Well, that was quite a story!" you tell yourself.
   "Tom was a decent guy.
   He deserves to have a break
   like discovering the value of the stone.
   Mr. Belden was a respectable fellow, too.
   Tom's mom was okay, too.
   Thank goodness she didn't over-protect Tom
   just because he was having a hard go of it.
   The author was pretty smart
   the way he put this story together."

An essay by Bill Martin, Jr.

A Turkey Speaks:

I have never understood
why anyone would
roast the turkey
and shuck the clams
and crisp the croutons
and shell the peas
and candy the sweets
and compote the cranberries
and bake the pies
and clear the table
and wash the dishes
and fall into bed,
when they could
sit back
and enjoy a

The Hodja is one of the most popular characters in Turkish folktales. His ways of solving problems are just as amusing to us as to the Turkish people. His name is pronounced Nas´-er-uh-din´ Hó-juh.

Three Fridays

A story by Alice Geer Kelsey,
pictures by Don Bolognese

There was just one day of each week that worried Nasr-ed-Din Hodja. On six days he was as free as a butterfly. He could talk with his friends in the market place or ride his donkey to a nearby village. He could work in the vineyards or go hunting in the hills. He could lounge in the coffee house or sit in the sun in his own courtyard. There was nothing to hurry him to be at a certain place at a certain time to do a certain thing.

But Friday was different. It was much different. That was the day when all good Mohammedans went to their mosques. Because Nasr-ed-Din Hodja, years before, had attended the school for priests, he was expected each Friday to mount the pulpit of the mosque at a certain time and preach a sermon. That was all very well when he had something to say, but there were many Fridays when his mind was as empty as that of his own little gray donkey. It was one thing to swap stories with the men in the coffee house and quite another to stand alone in the high pulpit and talk to a mosque full of people. The men, each squatting on his own prayer rug on the floor, looked up at him with such solemn faces. Then there was the fluttering in the balcony behind the lattices, which told him that the women were waiting, too. Of course, the chanting, which came before the sermon, was not hard because all the men joined in that, bowing till they touched their foreheads to the floor in the Nemaz. But the sermon — that was hard.

One Friday he walked more slowly than ever through the cobblestoned streets of Ak Shehir. He saw the veiled women slipping silently past him on their way to the latticed balcony of the mosque to hear his sermon. But what sermon? He stopped at the mosque door to leave his shoes. He pattered with the other men across the soft thick rugs. But they could squat on the rugs, while he had to climb into the high pulpit.

Perhaps the beauty of the mosque would give
him an idea. He looked up at the blues and reds
and whites of the intricate tracery on the ceiling,
but not a thought came. He looked at the rich
yellows and reds of the mosaics[1] on the walls,
but there was no help there. He looked at the
men's faces staring up at him. He heard the tit-
tering in the latticed balcony where the veiled
women sat. He must say something.

[1] pictures made from colored
pieces of stone

"Oh, people of Ak Shehir!" He leaned on the pulpit and eyed them squarely. "Do you know what I am about to say to you?"

"No!" boomed from the rugs where the men squatted.

"No!" floated down in soft whispers from the latticed balcony, whispers not meant for any ears beyond the balcony.

"You do not know?" said Nasr-ed-Din Hodja, shaking his head and looking from one face to another. "You are sure you do not know? Then what use would it be to talk to people who know nothing at all about this important subject. My words would be wasted on such ignorant people."

With that, the Hodja turned and climbed slowly down the pulpit steps. His eyes lowered, he walked with injured dignity through the crowds of men. He slipped on his shoes at the mosque door, and was out in the sunshine — free until next Friday.

That day came all too soon. The Hodja mingled with the crowds going to the mosque. His coarse, home-knit stockings pattered across the deep colorful rugs. He climbed the steps to the high pulpit. He looked down at the sea of solemn faces. He heard the rustling behind the lattices of the balcony. He had hoped that this week he could think of a sermon, but the carvings of the doorway did not help him nor the embroidered hangings of the pulpit nor the pigeon fluttering and cooing at the window. Still, he must say something.

"Oh, people of Ak Shehir!" intoned the Hodja, gesturing with both hands. "Do you know what I am about to say to you?"

"Yes," boomed the men who remembered what had happened when they said "No" last week.

"Yes," echoed in soft whispers from the balcony.

"You know what I am going to say?" said the Hodja, shrugging first one shoulder and then the other. "You are sure you know what I am going to say? Then I need not say it. It would be a useless waste of my golden words if I told you something that you already knew."

The Hodja turned and again climbed down the pulpit steps. He picked his way with unhurried dignity among the men. He scuffed into his shoes and escaped into the sunshine. Another free week was ahead of him.

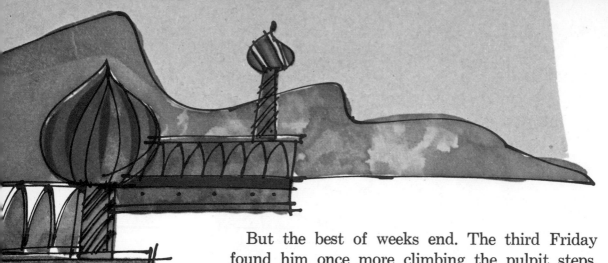

But the best of weeks end. The third Friday found him once more climbing the pulpit steps, with not a word saying in that solemn mosque. The ancient Arabic writing on the bright ceiling had no help for him. The flickering candles in the large round chandelier winked at him but said nothing. Even the big Koran[2] in front of him might have had blank pages instead of its fine Arabic words and its illuminated[3] borders. Men's faces looked up at him expectantly. Bright eyes peered through the lattices of the women's balcony. The time had come again when he must speak.

"Oh, people of Ak Shehir!" declaimed the Hodja as he groped helplessly for an idea. "Do you know what I am about to say to you?"

"No," came from those who were thinking of the last Friday.

"Yes," came from those who were thinking of the Friday before that.

"Some of you know and some of you do not know!" The Hodja rubbed his hands together and beamed down at the men. "How very fine! Now let those who know tell those who do not know!"

[2] holy book for Mohammedans
[3] decorated with fancy letters
and drawings

The Hodja was humming to himself as he came down from the pulpit, two steps at a time. He nodded and smiled as he threaded his way through the men. Some thought he bowed and smiled toward the latticed balcony, but others said the good Hodja would not have made so bold. He picked his own worn shoes from the rows and rows by the mosque door. The sunshine was warm and friendly. The birds were singing, and there was the fragrance of hawthorn blossoms in the air.

The Hodja had not a worry in the world — not till another Friday should come around.

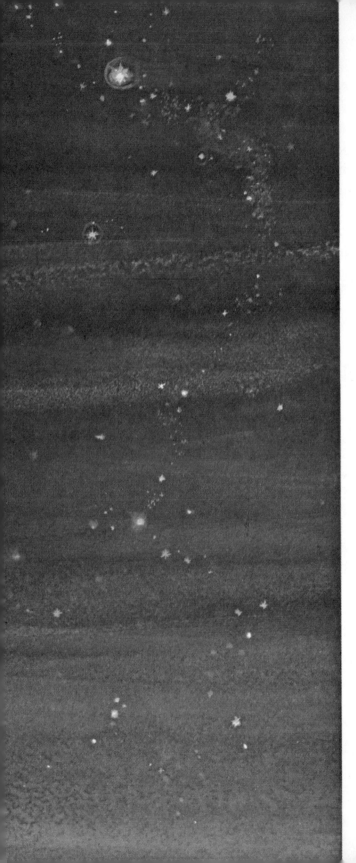

Silver

Slowly, silently, now the moon
Walks the night
    in her silver shoon;
This way, and that,
    she peers, and sees
Silver fruit upon silver trees;
One by one the casements catch
Her beams beneath
    the silvery thatch;
Couched in his kennel, like a log,
With paws of silver sleeps the dog;
From their shadowy cote
    the white breasts peep
Of doves in a silver feathered sleep;
A harvest mouse goes
    scampering by,
With silver claws, and silver eye;
And moveless fish
    in the water gleam,
By silver reeds in a silver stream.

A poem by Walter de la Mare

Something Told the Wild Geese

Something told the wild geese
   It was time to go.
Though the fields lay golden
   Something whispered, "Snow."
Leaves were green and stirring,
   Berries, luster-glossed,
But beneath warm feathers
   Something cautioned, "Frost."
All the sagging orchards
   Steamed with amber spice,
But each wild breast stiffened
   At remembered ice.
Something told the wild geese
   It was time to fly—
Summer sun was on their wings,
   Winter in their cry.

A poem by Rachel Field

Illustrations by Albert John Pucci   173

Under the wide and starry sky
Dig the grave and let me lie.
Glad did I live and gladly die,
And I laid me down with a will.

This be the verse that you grave for me:
Here he lies where he longed to be,
Home is the sailor, home from the sea,
And the hunter home from the hill.

Requiem
by Robert Louis Stevenson

The long canoe
Toward the shadowy shore,
One...two...
Three...four...
The paddle dips,
Turns in the wake,
Pauses, then
Forward again,
Water drips
From the blade to the lake.
Nothing but that,
No sound of wings;
The owl and bat
Are velvet things.
No wind awakes,
No fishes leap,
No rabbits creep
Among the brakes.

The long canoe
At the shadowy shore,
One...two...
Three...four...
A murmur now
Under the prow
Where rushes bow
To let us through.
One...two...
Upon the shore,
Three...four...
Upon the lake,
No one's awake,
No one's awake,
One...
Two...
No one,
Not even
You.

Lullaby

A poem by Robert Hillyer,
pen and ink drawing
by Sylvie Selig

The Ride-By-Nights

This poem by Walter de la Mare
is most effective
when chanted mysteriously
as a choral reading.

Up on their brooms the Witches stream,
Crooked and black in the crescent's gleam,
One foot high, and one foot low,
Bearded, cloaked, and cowled, they go.
'Neath Charlie's Wain° they twitter and tweet,
And away they swarm 'neath the Dragon's feet,°
With a whoop and a flutter they swing and sway,
And surge pell-mell down the Milky Way.

° the Big Dipper

° a constellation
near the North Pole

Picture by Albert John Pucci

RAIN IN SUMMER

by Henry Wadsworth Longfellow

How beautiful is the rain!
After the dust and heat,
In the broad and fiery street,
In the narrow lane,
How beautiful is the rain!

How it clatters along the roofs,
Like the tramp of hoofs!
How it gushes and struggles out
From the throat of the overflowing spout!
Across the window-pane
It pours and pours;
And swift and wide,
With a muddy tide,
Like a river down the gutter roars
The rain, the welcome rain!

Do You Fear the Force of the Wind?

Do you fear the force of the wind,
The slash of the rain?
Go face them and fight them,
Be savage again.
Go hungry and cold like the wolf,
   Go wade like the crane:
The palms of your hands will thicken,
The skin of your cheek will tan,
You'll grow ragged and weary and swarthy,
   But you'll walk like a man!

by Hamlin Garland

178

Last Song

To the Sun
Who has shone
   All day,
To the Moon
Who has gone
   Away,
To the milk-white,
Lily-white Star
A fond goodnight
Wherever you are.

by James Guthrie

A DAY AT HOME
in Uganda

When my little sister was born, I was sent to my grandfather's hut to sleep. The parents kept only the youngest child with them at night. The rest of the children slept away from home — boys with their grandfather, girls with their grandmother. The grandparents instructed their grandchildren in the tribal ways that a child in Uganda must learn in growing up. At daybreak, all children returned to their parents' hut to do their chores. My job was to nurse and look after the baby while my parents worked in the fields.

*Early
in the morning
my father
put out the animals
that had spent
the night
in our hut.
Then he went
to work.
My mother
joined him
after she
had cleaned up
the animals' mess
and had fed
the baby.*

An essay by Joseph A. Lijembe, with water colors by Willi Baum

On my arrival at sunrise from my grandfather's hut, I stirred up the fire in the fireplace so my mother could make breakfast. If the fire had gone out during the night, I went to other homes looking for fire. My breakfast was *bujeni,* the remains of last night's supper, but mother made cornmeal porridge for my father. Before going to work in the garden, my mother instructed me: "Do not leave the home unguarded for fear of thieves. Feed the baby when she cries. Guard the chickens from wild cats and the chicks from wild birds. And be helpful to visitors and strangers." She promised to bring me a fruit or a potato when she came home that night.

Mother filled our water jug at the river each morning. We used it carefully so it would last the day.

As soon as my mother left, I swept the floor, ground millet to make porridge for my baby sister, and prepared and cooked bananas. Whenever the baby awakened, I fed her. If she didn't want to eat, I took a handful of porridge and poured it into her mouth. But best of all, I joined the other boys and girls who were also nurses. As soon as our parents were out of sight and the babies were asleep, we met at an agreed upon place, carrying the sleeping babies with us. We either tied the babies to our backs or left them on the ground, sleeping as we played games and make-believe play such as hide-and-seek, imitating Mother at cooking, death ceremonies, riddles, house-building with corncobs, and harvesting.

Evening was a favorite time for all children of the village to come together to play. This included older boys and girls who had worked in the fields all day. We played until dark. As soon as one child was called home, the games came to an end.

When my mother returned from work in the evening, she checked to see if I had done my duties well. She inspected the house and also the baby. If the baby's eyes were red, she would know that the baby had cried a lot during the day. If the gourd was still full of porridge, she would know that I had not fed the baby as often as I was supposed to. Then I would be reported to my father who would decide the punishment and who also would inflict it. If all had gone well, my mother would feed the baby, lay her at a place to rest, and begin to prepare our evening meal. And I would be released to go play with the other children.

Later when my sister grew older and could care for herself, we were separated in all of our activities — even eating. My sister and other girls in the village ate together, visiting a different house each evening for their meal. They usually sat near the cooking place and were supervised by the mother in the home. We boys in the village ate our evening meal together, also visiting a different house each night. We moved from home to home until each home of the members of the group had been visited. In this way we came to appre-

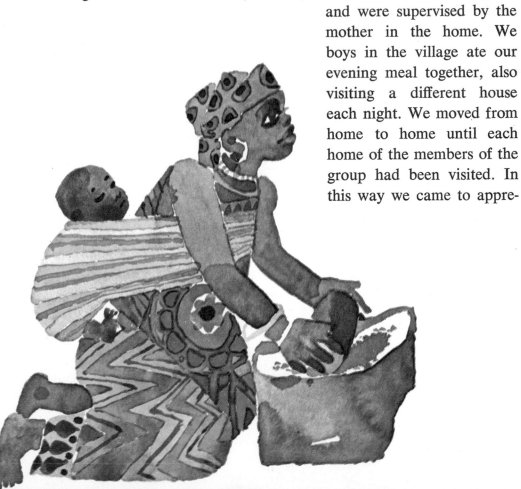

ciate or dislike the treatment given children in the different homes in our neighborhood. We ate in a different room from the girls, and we were unsupervised unless the father in the home happened to be around. Our eating manners were taught to us by our grandfathers in whose homes we slept at night.

Another duty of mine was collecting and carrying firewood. I hated this job because gathering firewood was a girl's work. But my mother refused me food if I didn't bring firewood during the day, so I had no choice but to do it.

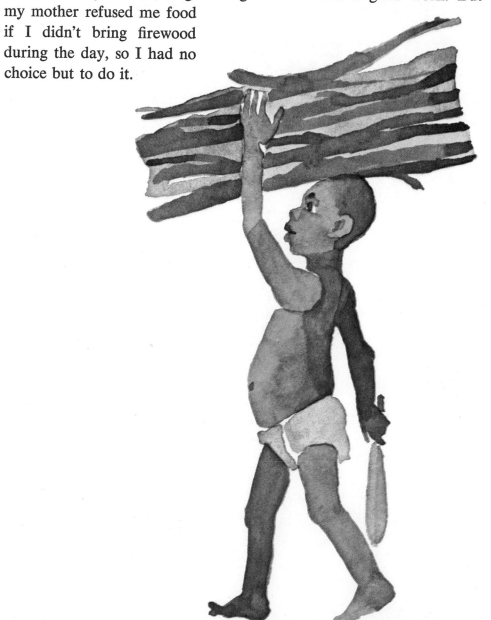

*I was afraid
of "night-runners"
and "ghosts"
and wild beasts
which my parents said
would get me
if I didn't obey.*

Fear played an important part in my growing up. Whenever I failed to do my work, my father gave me a good beating.

Once I helped myself to a piece of roasted meat that my mother was keeping for visitors. When she discovered that the hidden treasure had been eaten without her permission, she threatened to throw me out into the dark where the wild beasts could get me. One of the most dreaded animals in my childhood was a dead snake. It was believed that a dead snake wrapped around a child's waist for the night would cure him of bed-wetting.

plugging into meanings

An essay by Bill Martin, Jr.,
sculpture by Ralph Moxcey,
photograph by Bob O'Shaughnessy

Sometimes reading gives
new life to old meanings.
It gives you a chance
to interrelate
and reorganize old meanings
in ways that come off
new and fresh.
You may find this happening
when you read
Our Country 'Tis of Thee
in the choral reading section
of this book.
The structure of this selection,
beginning with the landing
of the Pilgrims
and following through
to the present time,
may give wholeness
and make new sense
out of things
you have been reading and hearing.
You also may discover
that the paintings used
in *Our Country 'Tis of Thee*
add information to the script.
Pictures often extend and refine
the meaning of the sentences
in a story
and deserve thoughtful viewing.

It will be interesting to see your response
to the poems and songs in this section.
Sometimes a poem or song, just by rhythm and melody,
gives more meaning than cold facts,
for in the pulse of the song or poem,
we often find the pulse or heartbeat of people.

You may have been led to believe
that when you read a book,
you are searching mainly for facts and author meanings.
This is partly true, but it is also partly untrue.
You also need to find your own feelings and ideas.
You have a storehouse of notions and ideas and feelings within you
that must be brought into play
as you search through sentences in a book for author meanings.

The place between author meanings and your meanings
is where the action lies.

A good reader learns to respect his own ideas and feelings
just as readily as he respects other people's—
including the author's of a book.
This does not mean that you can ignore the author's point of view.
You will want to know what he is thinking and feeling,
but merely because you discover his expressions
doesn't make them more worthwhile
than those that are bouncing around inside your head.

This ability to go into the reading of a selection
with eyes and hearts open to the interplay
of you and the author (and the artist)
is what reading is all about.
And reading really becomes worthwhile
when you come upon one line or one phrase
or one idea in an entire book
that adds to your storehouse of experiences
that mark you as you and not as just part of a mob.

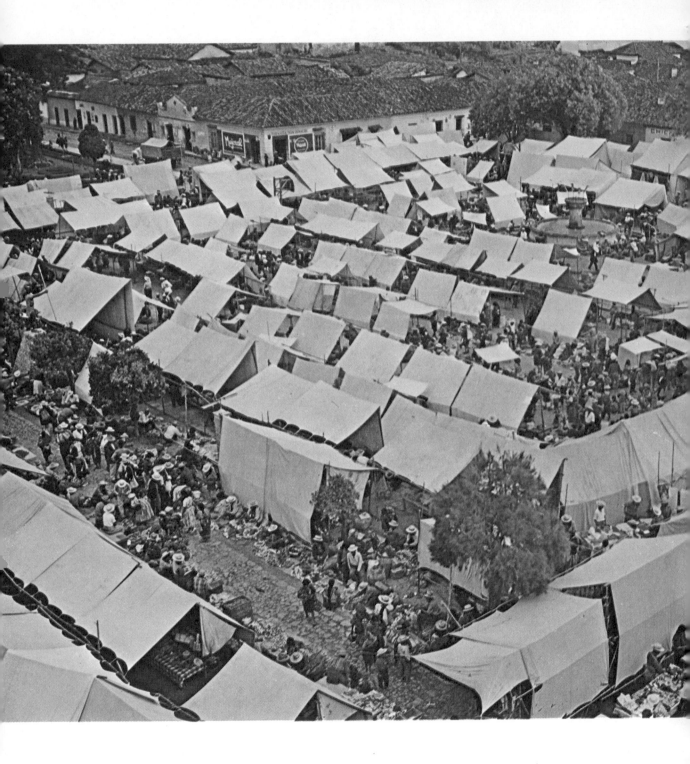

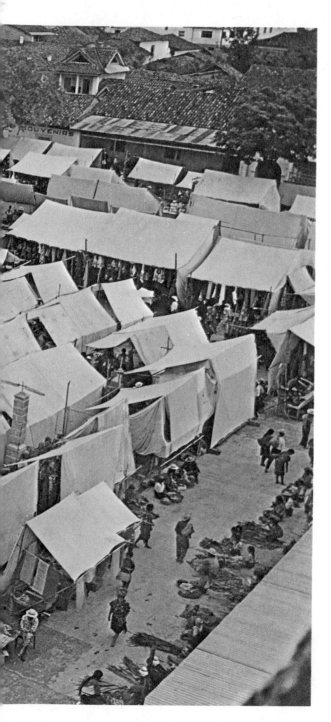

Guatemalan Market

Article and photographs by Peter Buckley

The marketplace in Chichicastenango is very important. It is so important that the entire town is built around it. The marketplace is a large square. Five days a week the square is empty, but on two days a week—market days—the square fills with people early in the morning. They spread their wares in the appointed places, then put up awnings to protect their goods from rain. Sudden rain storms, coming from the mountains, are a common occurrence in Chichicastenango.

Mountain people coming to market rise long before the sun is up and start their way down narrow mountain paths with their wares packed on their backs and shoulders. Those who live along lakes often travel part of the way to market in canoes. From wherever they come and from whatever distance, the people always arrive before eight o'clock in the morning. The market opens at eight.

Children rarely come to the market, perhaps only once or twice a year. When they do reach the marketplace after a two or three hour walk through the mountains, the children are shy because they are not used to seeing so many people all at once. The youngest babies are carried, strapped to their mother's backs.

For some, getting to market is not easy. Consider a man who lives forty miles from Chichicastenango. He leaves his small mountain village, laden with heavy earthen cooking pots which he hopes to sell. He also carries his tent, a little firewood, a sleeping mat and blankets, a water flask, an oil lamp, and a raincoat. He walks throughout one day, sleeping at night by the side of the mountain path. It takes another day and night for him to reach the market. If he is lucky, he will sell his pots before he starts his long walk home at the close of the third day.

Wares are set out on mats in the marketplace to be seen by those who are coming to buy. Many of those who buy goods are also sellers who have brought their own products to market. Consequently, a buyer often prefers to trade something he has for what he wants. Little money changes hands in the marketplace. As long as a man owns something he can use in trade, he has no need for money.

A fisherman from a lake village may offer five fish for a bag of corn that a mountain farmer is selling. The two men argue and discuss for a long time before they finally come to an agreement. Arguing and discussing are an important part of doing business in Chichicastenango.

If a holiday falls on the same date as market day, more people than usual come to Chichicastenango. The trading and buying ends at noon, and everyone gathers close to see the festivities.

Masked dancers dressed like Spaniards appear to entertain the crowd. They dance the story of the Spanish invasion of Central America more than four hundred years ago. The dance helps people who cannot read learn the history of their country. When the dance is over, the crowd thins out and starts for home.

Brighty stood waiting
for his food,
and as he waited
a speck of snow
fell on his nose.
A few flakes touched the fire,
made little hisses,
and were gone.
But away from the fire,
on bushes and junipers,
they hung like tiny white stars.

BRIGHTY

A story by Marguerite Henry, pictures by Wesley Dennis

Brighty walked
to the very edge of the cliff
and thrust his head out
into space.
He caught a few flakes
and tasted them on his tongue.
They were something new
and delicious.

In silence
the burro and the man
ate their meager lunch.
The wind rose
and a whirl of snow
swooped into the shelter,
powdering the man
hunched over his coffee.
He leaped to his feet
in panic.

He had never climbed
the north wall of the canyon
before.
In a snowstorm
he would need the burro
more than ever.

"I dreamt this blizzard
last night!"
he called out in alarm.
"I dreamt
the law was after me.
They trailed my footprints.
I got to go on!"

Quickly he shook the blanket
free of snow,
wrapped his skillet
and coffeepot
and the beaver pelts inside,
stuffed cold biscuits
in his pocket.
He threw the pack on Brighty
and jerked the ropes
around his belly.

Then he turned
to pick up the tin can
with the pebbles,
but there was no need to use it.

Brighty was already
out of reach.
He had set
the compass in his mind
for the North Rim.
Up ahead in the snow clouds
there would be
another kind of man,
a gentle man,
waiting to welcome him.

He bent his head
to the climb,
and at first
the snow was pleasant
to his face,
and he went with steady stride.
But as they climbed higher,
a wild mass of white
billowed into the canyon.
It closed in
on the figures toiling
up the wall
and muffled all sound
until the dead stillness
threw terror into the man.
He cried out,
and the words he cried were,
"Bright Angel! Bright Angel!"

Brighty had no ears
for the rasping voice.
He was completely baffled
by his first snow.

One moment
it was a frosted star
to taste on the tongue,
and the next,
a whipsnap of lightning
trying to blind him.

Gruntingly,
he defied the stinging lashes.
He groped with his feet
and used the pack as a feeler,
scraping it along the walls.
He gained a dozen yards
and stopped to catch his breath,
and another dozen yards
while the snow sifted down
into his ears
and through his coat to the skin.

On turns of the trail,
his head took the full fury
of the storm.
But his feet were sure,
testing the slippery rocks
for toeholds,
and inch by inch,
ledge by ledge,
moving him on.

At a stopping place
Jake Irons caught up
and clutched
Brighty's ropelike tail
to pull himself along.

*Without knowing who the man is or how he came to possess Brighty,
you will sense in this excerpt from* Brighty of the Grand Canyon
*the depth of evil in Jake Irons. Isn't it interesting that a man's treatment
of an animal tends to reveal his character?*

Before,
it had been
the man's desperate urge
to top out.[1]
Now it was the burro's.
He moved steadily upward,
letting his tail be a towrope,
letting it pull the man
as if he were a dead thing—
a sled or a log.
Hoofprints and footprints
were interlocking now,
and relentlessly
the wind and the snow
were erasing them both.
The way steepened
into rocky steps,
and Brighty knew
that he had come
to the Devil's Backyard.
The storm had muffled the noise
of Ribbon Falls
and Roaring Springs.
He had gone right by
without hearing their din.
He stumbled on a tree root
and almost fell
to the rocks below,
but the tree itself caught him.

Again the man cried out,
"Bright Angel! Bright Angel!"

But only the wind replied.

The sky darkened
with fast-moving clouds,
and the wind spiraled upward
into the clouds.
It sucked out more snow
and blew it over the rocks
until they had no shape at all.
It buried the trail, too,
as if it had never been.
And still Brighty trudged on
in his own peculiar way,
sometimes
almost crawling on his knees,
sometimes
taking the steps at a leap.

The man groaned,
"Whoa! Whoa! I can't breathe!"

But Brighty was a creature
homing,
a creature who must go on
in spite of ice and snow.
He could no longer see the way
in front of him,
but the pattern was fixed
in his mind.
The snowflakes melted
on his eyelashes
and stung hotly when he blinked,
then froze into tiny icicles.
Ice formed, too,
on the feathers[2] of his legs
and cut his pasterns[3]
as he walked.

[1] to reach the top of the canyon

[2] hair on back of leg below knee
[3] lower leg from knee to ankle

202

And still he kept on,
slipping, struggling,
feet and muscles aching,
lungs burning.
When he stopped to blow,
he heard the hollow voice crying,
"Food! Food! I'm starving!"

He glanced behind
and saw Irons huddled
into his coat,
gnawing on a frozen biscuit.
Deliberately he ran away
from the man.

In panic at being left alone,
Irons dropped his biscuit,
scrambled after Brighty,
groped for the tail,
caught it,
pulled himself up.
And now
hoofprints and footprints
interlocking again,
and the two creatures
all shrouded in snow.

As Brighty climbed onward,
he was aware that the trail
had begun to widen out.
He no longer needed
to hug the wall.
There were trees
on both sides now,

and the slope was gentler.
The struggle was almost over.

With Irons hanging on,
he jog-trotted the homestretch.

And when at last
he topped the rim,
he seemed to rout the storm.
The snow thinned,
ending abruptly,
and a soft mist rolled in
over the forest.

Suddenly a burst of sun
pierced the mist
and flung a rainbow,
like a triumphant arch of victory,
across the sky.

A delicious home-feeling
welled up in Brighty.
He wanted to run, to bray.

In spite of his weariness,
he was conscious
of an old remembered joy.
He saw ahead
the trees that Uncle Jimmy
had marked with a notch
and a slit.
He, Brighty,
had packed the hatchet
to mark these very trees!
He had completed the journey.

This spot of earth was Home.

Through aisles of aspen and pine,
Brighty headed
for Uncle Jim's cabin.

He ignored the man's pull
on his tail
and the whining cry behind.

His small hoofs, caked with ice,
shuffled in and out of the snow
with rhythmic strength.
He could feel rope burns
on his sides
where the straps had rubbed,
and his pack
had grown very heavy,
but there was happy purpose
in his step.

Confidently he entered the lane
winding down into the meadow.

But now as his eyes saw it,
he stopped dead.
A chill of fear swept over him.
The meadow was a glaze of white,
a sealed-in land,
all emptiness.
There was no sign of life
anywhere.
No creature stirred,
no man nor mule nor hound.
Not even a bird.
Everything had changed.
Where green grass had been,
there was instead
this smooth crystal sea.
And the cabin
was most changed of all.
It looked littler,
and it crouched down
in the corner of the meadow
like some white-haired crone[4]
with window-glass eyes.

Brighty stood helpless
in the quiet world of white.
Except for the black smudges
of his eyes,
he was snow-frosted, too,
like the meadow and the trees
and the little cabin.

The rainbow had faded,
and the low sun threw
only the palest of shadows

across the snow.
Slowly Brighty shuffled
toward the cabin.
He stopped
in front of the porch
and sounded a long-drawn bray.
His ears tipped forward,
listening.
But there was no
answering sound.
All he heard
was his heart beating,
and all he saw
was a spume of snow churning
in a little gust of wind.

The cabin door remained closed.

As the silence continued,
Irons came alive.
He let go Brighty's tail
and glanced up
at the cabin chimney
to make sure
the gray wisp above it
was cloud, not smoke.
Then he stamped
onto the porch
and knocked loudly
on the door.
He waited a moment,
his breath making
a hoarse whisper
in the stillness.

[4] a withered old woman

Then turning sideways,
he threw his body
against the door.
It flew open so easily
he fell sprawling on his face.

Brighty stepped in over him
and halted in bewilderment.
The place seemed colder
than the out-of-doors.
A hat and a jacket
hung on a wall,
but the smells they gave off
were old and faint.
He brayed
to bring the place alive,
but all it did
was to stir Jake Irons.

The man sat up,
rubbing his shins
while he stared intently
around the room
as if his eyes
might be playing tricks.
He picked himself up
and pushed at the walls
to make sure
they were real.
When they did not budge,
he closed the door behind him
and gave Brighty a jolt
with his knee.
"Not bad, jughead,"
he laughed harshly.
"Not half bad!"

Still remembering his dream,
he shoved a trunk-sized box
against the door
and then looked about.
He noted the readiness
of the room—
the bunk made up,
the logs stacked
beside the fireplace,
the canned goods lined up
store-neat,
and the kerosene lamp
with wick trimmed and waiting.
He blew on his hands
to warm them,
then picked up a log
and whittled chips for kindling.

He shook some kerosene
over the kindling
and laid on two logs.
Lighting the fire,
he cackled in relief
as the flames leaped up.

The heat felt good
to Brighty, too.
He gave himself a violent shake,
spraying snow
over the entire room.

"Get away from me,
you wet rat!"
Irons swung around
and struck Brighty
with the flat of his hand.

The startled burro backed up,
his hindquarters pushing
against a door
that squeaked open.
Irons shoved him on through
and peered into the darkness
of a small lean-to.
He grinned when he saw
the little room
was filled
with logs.
Not bothering
to remove Brighty's pack,
he stooped his way out,
letting the door whine shut
behind him.

Brighty paced restlessly
in the blackness.
He hungered
for light and warmth
and, most of all,
for food to quiet the pinching
of his belly.
He butted the door,
then turned and kicked it.
But suddenly he felt very tired,
and his kicking was half-hearted.

A boot came crashing
against the door
on the other side,
and a second boot,
and after a while
there were fainter noises—
tin dishes clicking together,
the slurping sound
of soup and coffee;
and after many minutes,
a watch being wound,
followed almost at once
by a steady snoring.

When the trembling
in Brighty's legs
had quieted,
he peeled a log with his teeth,
slowly chewing the bitter bark.

Then he nosed carefully
along the wall,
trying to find the green logs.

Halfway around,
his muzzle touched something
that gave to his bunting.
He bunted it again.
The thing was rough-textured
and it made a rustly noise.

He remembered that noise!
Oats!
Exquisite oats!

With a grunt of joy
he ripped a hole
in the gunny sack,
and then his muzzle
was in among the plump kernels.

A pleasant feeling
flowed into him
as his grinders made meal
of the grain,
and the juices in his mouth
turned it into a delicious mush.
He lipped another mouthful

and another,
and after a while
he stopped eating,
his small belly satisfied.

A warmth surged
through his body.
With his forefeet
inside the bag,
in the snug little nest
he had made,
he, too, slept and snored.

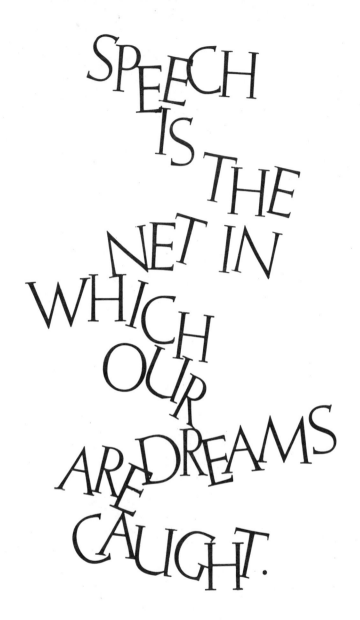

SPEECH IS THE NET IN WHICH OUR DREAMS ARE CAUGHT.

Designed by Art Ritter

How the
Little Old Woman
Did Her Marketing

A story by Hope Newell,
pictures by Ed Renfro

One day when the Little Old Woman was weeding her soup garden,
the pack peddler came along crying his wares.
"Any tacks, laces, nutmeg graters, ribbons,
mousetraps or buttons today?"
he cried.
The Little Old Woman shook her head.
"No," she said.
"I have no money to spare.
It is all I can do to make both ends meet."

"Any hairpins, cooking pots, calico, button hooks,
needles or spices?"
he cried.

But the Little Old Woman shook her head.
"No," she said.
"Today is market day,
and I must save my money to buy meat and bread for my supper."

"How about a pair of magnifying spectacles?"
asked the peddler.

"Magnifying spectacles!" exclaimed the Little Old Woman.
"And what may they be?"

"They are a very useful kind of spectacles,"
the peddler explained.
"When you wear them, everything looks twice as large as before."

"But what good are they?"
asked the Little Old Woman.
"Why should I want things to look twice as big as before?"

"That is easy to answer,"
the peddler replied.
"The larger things are, the more plainly you can see them."

"I never happened to think of that before,"
said the Little Old Woman.
"What you say is very true."

"Why not put the spectacles on,
and see for yourself how large things look?"
said the peddler.

"Well, I suppose it would do no harm to try them on," she said.
"But, mind you, I have no money to buy them."

"Just as you say," said the peddler.
He opened his pack and took out the magnifying spectacles.
The Little Old Woman put them on and looked at her soup garden.
She could hardly believe her eyes.
The cabbages looked twice as big.
The tomatoes looked twice as big.
Everything in the garden looked twice as big as it had before.
"How my vegetables have grown!"
exclaimed the Little Old Woman.
"And how plainly I can see them!
These are very fine spectacles indeed."

"They are quite cheap, too," said the peddler.
"If you should buy them,
I am sure they would come in very handy."

"That is just what I was thinking,"
the Little Old Woman replied.
"I will fetch you some money from my china teapot."
She hurried into the house
and took some money from out of her china teapot
to pay for the spectacles.
After the peddler had gone, she said to herself:
"I should like to look at the soup garden
through these spectacles again.
But first I must go to market
and buy some bread and meat for my supper."

As she was getting ready to go to the market, she thought:
"I will take the spectacles with me
and wear them while I am doing my marketing.
I will be able to see more plainly,
and I will get more for my money."
So the Little Old Woman put the magnifying spectacles
in her market basket and took them with her.
After she reached the market,
she put on the spectacles so she could see more plainly.
When she went to buy her bread, she said to the baker:
"What fine rolls you have today!
They are nearly as large as a loaf of bread.
One roll will be all I will need."
She bought one roll and put it in her market basket.
Then she went to buy her meat.
"What fine chops you have today," she said to the butcher.
"They are nearly as large as a whole roast.
One chop will be all I will need."
So she bought one chop and put it in her market basket.
As the Little Old Woman was coming home from market,
she said to herself:
"I have never bought so much bread and meat for so little money.
These spectacles are very useful indeed."
When she was home again, she set about preparing her supper.

She took the roll out of the market basket.
"This roll is too big for one meal," she thought.
"I will cut off a piece and save the rest for tomorrow."
After she had cut off a piece of the roll and put the rest away,
she took the chop out of her market basket.
"This chop is too big also," she thought.
"I will cut off a piece and save the rest for tomorrow."
So she cut off a piece of the chop and put the rest of it away.
When she had prepared her supper,
the Little Old Woman took off her magnifying spectacles.
She put them away carefully and then sat down to eat.
She looked at the piece of roll.
It was no bigger than a thimble.
She looked at the piece of chop.
It was no bigger than a thimble either.
"Mercy!" cried the Little Old Woman.
"What has happened to my supper?
There is not enough left to feed a mouse!"

She began to look for the rest of her supper.
She looked at her plate.
She looked under her plate.
But she did not find it.
She looked on the table.
She looked under the table.
But she did not find the rest of her supper.

After she had looked everywhere, she said:
"This is very strange.
Something seems to be wrong,
and I must use my head to find out what it is."
So she tied a wet towel around her forehead
and sat down with her forefinger against her nose
and shut her eyes.
She used her head and used her head.
Pretty soon she found out what to do.
"What a silly Old Woman I am!" she said.
"How can I find my supper when I cannot see plainly?

I must put on my magnifying spectacles."
The Little Old Woman got her magnifying spectacles
and put them on.
Then she came back to the table.
She looked at her plate,
and there she saw her supper as plainly as anything.
As she sat down to eat, she said to herself:
"It was very wise of me to put on my magnifying spectacles.
Now I see my supper very plainly.
And what a fine big supper it is, to be sure!
I am afraid I shall not be able to eat half of it."

SNOW

BOUND

The sun that brief December day
Rose cheerless over hills of gray,
And, darkly circled, gave at noon
A sadder light than waning moon. . . . . .
Unwarmed by any sunset light
The gray day darkened into night,
A night made hoary with the swarm
And whirl-dance of the blinding storm. . . . . .
So all night long the storm roared on:
The morning broke without a sun. . . . . .
And, when the second morning shone,
We looked upon a world unknown,
On nothing we could call our own. . . . .
No cloud above, no earth below, —
A universe of sky and snow!

A poem by John Greenleaf Whittier

BLIZZARD HITS WESTERN STATES

AIR FORCE'S "OPERATION FEEDLIFT" BALKED BY CONTINUING BLIZZARD

CHICAGO, Jan. 20—One of the worst storms in memory hit Montana, eastern Washington, Utah, Nevada, Wyoming, Colorado and the Dakotas today in the form of blizzards, floods and bitter Arctic cold.

Some areas were buried under as much as 80 inches of snow, which forced the closing of schools and blocked highways. Freezing winds blew roofs off buildings, smashed windows and ripped down power and telephone lines. Brief gusts of the blizzard winds reached speeds as high as 95 miles an hour in parts of Montana and the Dakotas.

Many families and thousands of farm animals were reported marooned by snow-blocked roads.

Senator Arthur V. Watkins of Utah urged the Commanding General of the Sixth Army at San Francisco to send immediate aid to combat winter conditions that were "endangering human life and livestock and game."

The cold wave, moving down from Canada, sent the temperature plunging to 36 degrees below zero at Frazer, Colorado, while Big Piney, Wyoming, registered 34 below.

'FLYING BOXCARS' TO DELIVER HAY TO STORM AREA

DENVER, Jan. 22—The Air Force announced that it plans to begin "Operation Feedlift" in an effort to save tens of thousands of cattle and sheep stranded in the snow-swept Western rangelands. An Air Force spokesman said that twelve C–82 "Flying Boxcars" stationed at Fallon, Nevada, would fly 1,000 tons of hay and cottonseed cake to snowbound sheep and cattle. A "Flying Boxcar" can carry about five tons of hay on each trip.

However, bad flying weather created by the heavy snow and driving winds delayed for at least one day all efforts to deliver the feed to the hungry animals.

The blizzard became so dangerous to human life and livestock today that the Governor of Utah declared a state of emergency. He said that the snow, whipped by high winds, had blocked all roads into Utah's west-central rangelands, causing the plight of the state's 1,616,000 sheep to become "dismal."

Army Sends Aid

The Governor of South Dakota asked the U.S. Army to send all available snow-moving equipment and bulldozers to clear snow-blocked roads into the rangeland areas of that state. Thousands of animals in South Dakota are facing starvation, the Governor said.

Livestock experts in Wyoming have estimated that the blizzard had already killed 55,200 head of cattle and over 100,000 sheep in Wyoming alone. There was no estimate available of the number of animals that have been killed by the blizzard in Utah, Colorado and Nebraska, but ranchers in those states have found thousands of cattle and sheep dead in the deep snow drifts.

Senator Joseph C. O'Mahoney of Wyoming praised the Air Force's "Operation Feedlift," but he said today that the only real answer was to clear the highways of drifts so that feed in large amounts could be trucked to the isolated herds of livestock.

The Senator, after declaring that the storm was "the most severe experienced in the Rocky Mountain area within the mem-

Photo by Carl Iwasaki, *Life* Magazine © Time Inc.

Range cattle had no way to escape the onslaught of the blizzard that hit the Western states yesterday and left thousands of animals and people stranded. This cow numbly awaits help.

ory of living man," said he would offer a bill to Congress to repay the Army and Air Force for any money they might spend helping the stricken Western states keep their roads clear of drifting snow.

Effort to Unblock Roads

A spokesman for the Fifth Army agreed with Senator O'Mahoney of Wyoming that primary efforts should be directed toward opening up snow-blocked roads, "because we just don't have enough planes or time to feed all the livestock by air." He ex-

plained that 500 flights a day would be necessary to feed the 100,000 starving cattle in just one Nebraska county alone.

In the meantime, the blizzard continues. More snow, driven by bitterly cold winds, was falling on Montana, Colorado, Utah, Nevada, Nebraska and the Dakotas. And the weather forecasters offered no cheering prospects today. The seven-state region is slated for still more snow, winds and sub-zero weather as another mass of frigid air moves down out of Canada.

225

'OPERATION FEEDLIFT' IN FULL SWING AT LAST

FELLON, NEV., Jan. 26—"Operation Feedlift" is now in full operation, even though flying conditions are described by Army pilots as being worse than any they ever encountered in Alaska.

In order to get the hay to snowbound cattle in seven Western states, the pilots of the C–82 "Flying Boxcars" have used skip-bombing methods for dropping feed to starving cattle and people.

One pilot in the Air Transport Service said, "We can drop Army C-rations right on the front steps of a farmhouse or put a bale of hay right under the nose of a steer with our skip-bombing methods."

How It's Done

Most of the hay drops are made at an altitude of about 50 feet. One danger of flying so low is that the plane's propellers churn up the fine powdered snow and make a blizzard around the plane.

Another danger is the flocks of turkeys in the storm area. When the turkeys hear a plane, they "fly off in all directions," said one pilot, and they could do great damage to the planes if they were to fly into the cockpit windows or into one of the propellers.

The planes usually carry a local rancher as a spotter. When the rancher spots an isolated herd of cattle or flock of sheep, he points it out to the plane's pilot. The pilot takes the plane down to the "target."

In the rear of the plane, a crew member stands by the open door ready to kick out a few bales of hay to the cattle. He wears goggles to protect his eyes against the flying haydust and a rope around his waist to keep from being pulled out of the plane by wind suction. When he receives the message from the pilot, he kicks out a few bales of hay, and then the plane goes soaring off to find another isolated herd.

Army Gives Aid to the Snowbound

DENVER, Jan. 29—The Air Force today expanded its efforts to airlift feed to the approximately 2,000,000 stranded and starving cattle and sheep in seven Western states.

In Nevada during the 24-hour period up until noon yesterday, the "Flying Boxcars" of the Air Transport Service had dropped more than 82 tons of hay to the herds of cattle in that state.

Meanwhile, "Operation Feedlift" has been renamed "Operation Snowbound." Officials said

Photo by Carl Iwasaki, *Life* Magazine © Time Inc.

A storm-stricken rancher signals his plight by blocking out the word COAL in the snow. Now he and his family can only wait and hope that a passing Air Force Transport plane will spot and respond to their message.

ka, and Martin, South Dakota, as well as several towns in the North Platte and Grand Island areas of Nebraska.

Federal Efforts

Army, Navy and National Guard units, along with Red Cross workers and building contractors, have hurled all available ground equipment into "Operation Snowbound." Helicopters, caterpillar tractors, bulldozers, rotary snowplows, "weasels" (track-equipped vehicles capable of plowing their way through deep snow) and jeeps pulling huge, quickly built sleds have been used to re-establish communications with isolated communities and to distribute feed to stricken livestock. Army officials in Utah have discussed the use of tanks with flame-throwers to melt snowdrifts and clear roads.

Plight of Livestock

In spite of such massive efforts, however, ranchers feared their livestock losses would total 50 per cent of their herds. Such a loss would amount to about $30,-000,000.

"And unless we can get feed and water very soon," said one livestock expert, "the loss will probably be even greater." He explained that calving time is only a month away, and the ranchers fear a tremendous loss not only of new stock but of breeding cows as well.

Meanwhile, the Weather Bu-

that the purpose of the operation now is to get emergency help to people as well as to livestock.

In Washington, the Secretary of the Interior said that scores of deaths had already been reported in the disaster areas, and that from now on the number-one problem of Federal Agencies would be the relief and rescue of the hundreds of persons snowbound on their farms and ranches and in the small communities which have been isolated by the storm.

To achieve this mission, "Operation Snowbound" has become the most far-flung rescue operation of its kind in history.

It has become a race with time. Many small communities are running out of food and fuel. Fifth Army Headquarters listed such communities as O'Neill, Nebras-

reau in Kansas City warned that a new storm is bearing down on the area. Since yesterday, temperatures have dropped to more than 40 degrees below zero in parts of Wyoming and Montana, while Carlin, Nevada, recorded the coldest temperature in the nation with a reading of 57 below zero.

The prediction of a new storm left Army officials grim. One said, "Only two inches of snow could stall this whole operation. We're working day and night to rescue as many snowbound people as we can before this new storm hits."

In Utah, schools were closed again, coal mining operations were discontinued, and many industries had to shut down. All planes were grounded, including those that had been carrying hay to stricken livestock. In addition, the Union Pacific Railroad reported that 45 of its trains were stalled or completely buried in the mountainous snowdrifts between Omaha and Pocatello, Idaho. Aboard the trains are 4,000 passengers.

The Red Cross in Douglas, Wyoming, was readying blankets and Army rations for air-shipment to the passengers on the stalled trains in that area.

In Green River, Wyoming, a Red Cross worker said that two of five babies removed from stalled trains there had pneumonia.

Two rotary snowplows trying to get to one of the stalled trains were caught by snowslides. It took the crews two hours to dig them out.

Damage Estimates

The most recent nationwide survey by the United Press showed that winter weather has already caused 579 deaths in all states since January 1, while property damage of all kinds totalled more than $236,000,000 for the same period.

The new blizzard was a heartbreaking blow to the ranchers in the region. Most of them had begun to hope that they could save "at least some" of their livestock.

It was feared by Federal livestock experts that the entire livestock industry of Utah would be wiped out unless the weather eased soon.

The Army in two weeks had cleared 43,704 miles of roads and reached 83,744 snowbound persons. "Now," said the General in charge of the operation, "we've got to start all over again."

NEW BLIZZARD BATTERS WEST

CHEYENNE, Feb. 5—A big new blizzard of snow and icy gale winds howled out of Canada today with blinding fury and spread across the storm-weary states of

Wyoming, Utah, Montana, Nevada, Colorado and Nebraska.

With winds ranging from 30 to 70 miles per hour, the new storm struck at helpless snowbound livestock and people of remote rural communities. The winds ripped down power and telephone lines and blocked roads and highways that were only recently cleared by the massive rescue efforts of the Army's "Operation Snowbound."

It meant that the backbreaking work to open roads and relieve the suffering of both humans and livestock will have to begin all over again.

Snowbound Flocks of Sheep to Get Dogs by Parachute

SALT LAKE CITY, Feb. 7 — "Operation Haylift" has now become "Operation Doglift."

An official in the Utah Civil Air Patrol said today that snowbound sheepherders in Utah were in desperate need of sheepdogs to protect their flocks of sheep from preying coyotes and wolves. The long period of deep snow has made finding food very difficult for the coyotes and wolves, so they have begun to raid the flocks boldly.

The sheepherders need dogs to stem these attacks.

Because land delivery of the dogs is now impossible in the snow-blocked areas, the Civil Air Patrol has decided to deliver the dogs by parachute.

Blizzard Victims Tell of Ordeal

NORTH PLATTE, NEB., Feb. 6 — Victims of the great Western blizzard told their stories today after having been freed by "Operation Snowbound" from many days and sometimes weeks of enforced isolation.

Ernest Hyden, who with his family of six had been snowbound on their ranch 20 miles south of Aimsworth for nearly a month, said:

"Our home was completely buried in snow. We couldn't get out of the house for three days. After we used up the firewood stored in the house, we broke up furniture and burned it to keep warm."

When the family finally dug its way out from under the snow, "it didn't do us much good," said Mr. Hyden. "The outside cellar, where we had lots of canned goods

Photo by Charles Steinheimer, *Life* Magazine © Time Inc.

A "Flying Boxcar" of the Air Transport Service drops bales of hay to stranded livestock in Nevada as part of the rescue efforts following the worst snowstorm in history.

stored, was buried under a 25-foot snowbank, so we couldn't get to it. But we did get firewood by sawing off the tops of fence posts that stuck up above the snow."

"But after three weeks," said Mr. Hyden's wife, Joy, "we were out of nearly everything. All we could do was sit there in that cold house, hungry, and think about all that food out there in the cellar that we couldn't get to."

A Civil Air Patrol ski-plane rescued the Hyden family yesterday and brought them to North Platte. The John P. Smith family, also snowbound for three weeks, made ample use of their corn-crib to survive. Said Mr. Smith, "We finally were able to dig a path to the corn-crib. We shelled corn all day, ate the corn and burned the cobs. We got awful sick of corn, but it saved us."

Norma Jean Webster, of Alliance, was one of many persons caught away from home by the storm and separated from their families for many weeks. Norma Jean, aged 12, was in school when the first blizzard hit. She has not been home since.

The Red Cross found her a place to stay in Alliance until the storm let up and snow-removal equipment opened up the road to the farm where the rest of the Webster family was trapped by the mountainous snowdrifts.

RELIEF IN SIGHT FOR STORM-WEARY WEST

DENVER, Feb. 11—The full force of "Operation Snowbound," with its hundreds of bulldozers, helicopters, planes, snowplows, tanks and weasels, is proceeding in the recently renewed battle to reach snowbound persons and isolated herds of livestock across the storm-ravaged six-state area.

Snow-barricaded railroad tracks in Nebraska and Wyoming were finally cleared yesterday and 28 stalled trains have been freed. Some of the trains had been stranded for days. Passengers had survived the ordeal by huddling together for warmth and eating Army rations dropped by planes.

The "digging-out" progress in the snowbound states has been so successful within the last few days that Federal officials, meeting in Washington, agreed that, with the exception of a few areas in Montana and Wyoming, the state of emergency has passed.

Photograph by Jerry Brimacombe Courtesy *Life* Magazine © Time Inc.

Desolate Beauty as the Great Blizzard Thaws

CHICAGO, Feb. 20—The winter-ravaged West was warmed by spring temperatures today. It was the first relief from the blizzards, snows, winds and sub-zero cold that the area has experienced in a month. In many areas the temperature shot up into the 50's and 60's.

But now, even as the Army continues its "Operation Snowbound," the warm weather and rapidly melting snow brings a threat of floods. The Kansas City Weather Bureau today issued a special warning of flood threats in Kansas, Missouri, Iowa and Nebraska.

Part II

responding to reading

As you have observed, this book is divided into two parts. The first 231 pages include selections and comments that help you understand what reading is all about. The next 153 pages include selections and comments that will help you weave what you read into your life. Reading a book only becomes important when that reading changes your notions about yourself and your life for the better. In Part II of this book, you will discover a variety of ways for using what you read.

An announcement by Bill Martin, Jr.

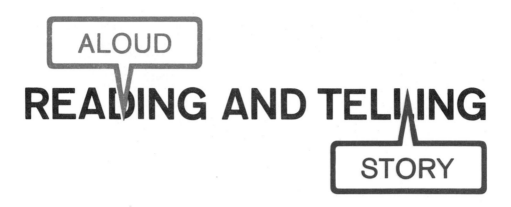

READING AND TELLING
ALOUD
STORY

An essay by Bill Martin, Jr.

There are four kinds of storytelling:

1) Telling a story of something that happened to you;
2) Making up a story about an event or a picture
   such as our Pictures for Storytelling;
3) Reading a story or poem aloud;
4) Telling in your own words a story that you have read
   in a book or heard someone else tell.

You will have opportunity to use all of these kinds
of storytelling in this book.

Ever since man invented sign language and spoken language,
he has been improving his ways of sharing his experiences
with his fellow men.
Nothing pleases him more than to entertain others
with a recitation of his own adventures.
There is a natural tendency, of course,
for the storyteller to do "a little boasting" in his storytelling
so that he, the hero, comes off better in the story
than he did in real life.

Sometimes the boasting about an adventure
becomes greater and greater each time the story is told,
so that the final result is a tall tale
such as *How Old Stormalong Captured Mocha Dick* on page 320.
Other times the storytelling is quiet and simple
such as Joseph Lijembe's telling of his African childhood on page 180.
Other times, the story is musical and poetic
like "Goody O'Grumpity " on page 237.

But however the storyteller chooses to recount his tale,
the main factor is his joy in the telling
and his ease in shaping the words and the sentences.
The storyteller who speaks readily,
knowing what he wants to say and how to say it,
has little trouble getting "in tune" with his audience.
The best way to gain ease in telling a story
is reading aloud or telling the story aloud
many times over,
so that every word and every sentence
comes off the tongue like an "old friend."
The story itself is an "old friend" to the storyteller.
He has chosen to tell it or read it because he loves it,
because he always finds delight in sharing it with others.
The storyteller knows that he is not "giving a show."
He is simply telling something that matters a lot to him.
Sometimes he makes up the story as he goes along,
but even so, he has thought seriously of what he wants to say.
He finds that his second telling is better than his first,
and that his third is better than his second.
Interestingly enough, his audience likes to hear his stories
more than once, too.

A Picture for Storytelling

Photograph by Art Kane

A Cliché

is what we all say
when we're too lazy
to find another way

and so we say

warm as toast,
quiet as a mouse,
slow as molasses,
quick as a wink.

Think.
Is toast the warmest thing you know?
Think again, it might not be so.
Think again: it might even be snow!
Soft as lamb's wool, fleecy snow,
a lacy shawl of new-fallen snow.

Listen to that mouse go
scuttling and clawing,
nibbling and pawing.
A mouse can speak
if only a squeak.

Is a mouse the quietest thing you know?
Think again, it might not be so.
Think again: it might be a shadow.
Quiet as a shadow,
quiet as growing grass,
quiet as a pillow,
or a looking glass.

Slow as molasses,
quick as a wink.
Before you say so,
take time to think.

Slow as time passes
when you're sad and alone;
quick as an hour can go
happily on your own.

A poem by Eve Merriam

Goody O'Grumpity

When Goody O'Grumpity baked a cake
The tall reeds danced by the mournful lake,
The pigs came nuzzling out of their pens,
The dogs ran sniffling and so did the hens,
And the children flocked by dozens and tens.

They came from the north, the east and the south
With wishful eyes and watering mouth
And stood in a crowd about Goody's door,
Their muddy feet on her sanded floor.

And what do you s'pose they came to do!
Why, to lick the dish when Goody was through!
And throughout the land went such a smell
Of citron and spice — no words can tell

How cinnamon bark and lemon rind,
And round, brown nutmegs grated fine
A wonderful haunting perfume wove,
Together with allspice, ginger and clove,
When Goody but opened the door of her stove.

The children moved close in a narrowing ring,
They were hungry — as hungry as bears in the spring;
They said not a word, just breathed in the spice,
And at last when the cake was all golden and nice,
Goody took a great knife and cut each a slice.

A poem by Carol Ryrie Brink

Who Was That Early Sodbuster?

A poem by Carl Sandburg

Who was that early sodbuster in Kansas?
He leaned at the gatepost and studied the horizon
and figured what corn might do next year
and tried to calculate why God ever made the grasshopper
and why two days of hot winds smother the life
out of a stand of wheat
and why there was such a spread between what he got for grain
and the price quoted in Chicago and New York.

Drove up a newcomer in a covered wagon:
"What kind of folks live around here?"
"Well, stranger, what kind of folks was there
in the country you come from?"
"Well, they was mostly a lowdown, lying, thieving,
gossiping, backbiting lot of people."
"Well, I guess, stranger,
that's about the kind of folks you'll find around here."

And the dusty gray stranger had just about blended
into the dusty gray cottonwoods in a clump on the horizon
when another newcomer drove up:
"What kind of folks live around here?"
"Well, stranger, what kind of folks was there
in the country you come from?"
"Well, they was mostly a decent, hardworking,
lawabiding, friendly lot of people."
"Well, I guess, stranger,
that's about the kind of folks you'll find around here."

And the second wagon moved off
and blended with the dusty gray cottonwoods on the horizon
while the early sodbuster leaned at his gatepost
and tried to figure why two days of hot winds
smother the life out of a nice stand of wheat.

comforting thoughts

a fish who had

swallowed an angleworm

found all too late

that a hook was nesting

in its midst ah me

said the poor fish

i am the most luckless

creature in the world

had you not pointed

that out said the worm

i might have supposed

myself a trifle

unfortunate

from *the lives and times of archy and mehitabel*
by don marquis

archie the cockroach
climbed upon a typewriter
one night
and found a paper in the machine
all ready for typing
so he jumped around the keys
to spell out this message
for humans

The Princess and the Vagabone

An Irish folktale
retold by Ruth Sawyer,
linoleum cuts by Eric Carle

ONCE IN THE GOLDEN TIME when an Irish king
sat in every province and plenty covered the land,
there lived in Connaught a grand old king with one daughter.
She was as tall and slender as the reeds that grow by Lough Erne,
and her face was the fairest in seven counties.
This was more the pity, for the temper she had
did not match it at all, at all;
it was the blackest and ugliest that ever fell
to the birthlot of a princess. She was proud, she was haughty;
her tongue had the length and the sharpness of the thorns
on a *sidheog* bush; and from the day she was born
till long after she was a woman grown, she was never heard to say
a kind word or known to do a kind deed to a living creature.

As each year passed, the King would think to himself:
"'Tis the New Year will see her better." But it was worse
instead of better she grew, until one day the King found himself
at the end of his patience, and he groaned aloud
as he sat alone, drinking his poteen.

"Faith, another man shall have her for the next eighteen years,
for, by my soul, I've had my fill of her!"

So it came about,
as I am telling ye,
that the King sent word
to the nobles
of the neighboring provinces
that whosoever would win
the consent of his daughter
in marriage
should have half of his kingdom
and the whole of his blessing.
On the day that she was eighteen,
they came: a wonderful procession
of earls, dukes, princes, and kings,
riding up to the castle gate,
　　a-courting.

The King made each one welcome
according to his rank;
and then he sent a serving-man
to his daughter,
bidding her come
and choose her suitor,
the time being ripe
for her to marry.
It was a courteous message
that the King sent,
but the Princess heard little of it.
Into the hall she flew
on the heels of the serving-man,
like a chicken hawk
after a bantam cock.

Her eyes burned with the anger
that was hot in her heart,
and she stamped her foot
in her father's face
until the rafters rang
with the noise of it.

"So, ye will be giving me away
for the asking—
to any of these blithering fools
who has a rag to his back
or a castle to his name?"

The King grew crimson at her words.
He was ashamed
that they should all hear
how sharp was her tongue;
moreover, he was fearsome
lest they should take to their heels
and leave him
with a shrew on his hands
for another eighteen years.
He was hard at work
piecing together a speech
when the Princess strode past him
to the first suitor in the line.

243

"At any rate,
   I'll not be choosing ye,
      ye long-legged corn crake,"
   and she gave him a sound kick
      as she went on to the next.
   He was a large man
   with a shaggy beard;
and, seeing how
the first suitor had fared,
he tried a wee bit of a smile
while his hand went out coaxingly.
She saw,
and the anger in her grew threefold.
She sprang at him,
digging the two of her hands
deep in his beard,
and then she wagged
his foolish head back and forth,
screaming: "Take that, and that,
ye old whiskered rascal!"

It was a miracle
that any beard was left on his face
the way that she pulled it.
But she let him go free at last
and turned to a thin-faced prince
with a monstrous long nose.
The nose took her fancy,
and she gave it a tweak,
telling the prince
to take himself home
before he did any damage with it.

The next one
she called "pudding-face"
and slapped his fat cheeks
until they were purple,
and the poor lad groaned
with the sting of it.

"Go back to your trough,
for I'll not marry a grunter,"
said she.

She moved swiftly down the line
in less time than it takes
for the telling.
It came to the mind
of many of the suitors
that they would be doing
a wise thing
if they betook themselves off
before their turn came;
as many of them
as were not fastened to the floor
    with fear
started away.
There happened to be
a fat, crooked-legged prince
from Leinster
just making for the door
when the Princess looked around.
In a trice
she reached out for the tongs
that stood on the hearth nearby,
and she laid it across his shoulders,
sending him spinning into the yard.

"Take that, ye old gander,
and good riddance to ye!"
she cried after him.

It was then
that she saw looking at her
a great towering giant of a man;
and his eyes burned through hers,
deep down into her soul.
So great was he
that he could have picked her up
with a single hand
and thrown her into the courtyard;
yet she felt no fear.
He was so handsome
that not a mortal fault
could she have found with him,
not if she had tried
for a hundred years.
The two of them
stood facing each other, glaring,
as if each would spring
at the other's throat
the next moment;
but all the while
the Princess was thinking
and thinking how wonderful he was,
from the top
of his curling black hair,
down the seven feet of him,
to the golden clasps on his shoes.

What the man was thinking I cannot be telling.
Like a breath of wind on smoldering turf,
her liking for him set her anger fierce-burning again.
She gave him a sound cuff on the ear, then turned,
and with a sob in her throat,
she went flying from the room,
the serving-men scattering before her
as if she had been a hundred million robbers on a raid.

And the King? Faith, he was dumb with rage.
But when he saw the blow that his daughter had given
to the finest gentleman in all of Ireland, he went after her
as if he had been two hundred million constables
on the trail of robbers.

"Ye are a disgrace and a shame to me,"
said he, catching her two hands
firmly; "and, what's more,
ye are a disgrace to my castle and my kingdom;
I'll not keep ye in it a day longer.
The first traveling vagabone who comes begging
at the door shall have ye for his wife."

"Will he?" said the Princess. She tossed her head
in the King's face and went to her chamber.

The next morning
a poor singing *sthronshuch* came to the castle
to sell a song for a penny or a morsel of bread.
The song that he sang was sweet, and the Princess listened
as Oona, the tirewoman, was winding strands
of her long black hair with golden thread.

> "The gay young wren sang over the moor.
>   'I'll build me a nest,' sang he.
> ' 'Twill have a thatch and a wee latched door,
>   For the wind blows cold from the sea.
> And I'll let no one but my true love in,
>   For she is the mate for me,'
>   Sang the gay young wren.

The wee brown wren by the hedgerow cried,
*   'I'll wait for him here,' cried she.*
'For the way is far and the world is wide,
*   And he might miss the way to me.*
Long is the time when the heart is shut,
*   But I'll open to none save he,'*
*   Sang the wee brown wren."*

A strange throb came
to the heart of the Princess
when the song was done.
She pulled her hair free
from the hands of the tirewoman.

"Get silver," she said;
"I would throw it to him."
And when she saw
the wonderment grow
in Oona's face,
she added:

"The song pleased me.
Can I not pay for what I like
without having ye look at me
as if ye feared
my wits had flown?
Go, get the silver!"

But when she pushed open
the grating and leaned far out
to throw the money,
the *sthronshuch* had gone.

Now the King had heard the song
as well as the Princess.
His rage was still with him,
and he lost no time
calling the vagabone inside.

"Ye are as fine a vagabone
as I could wish for," he said.
"Maybe ye are not knowing it,
but this day
ye are to be a bridegroom."
And the King went on
to tell him the whole tale.
The tale being finished,
the King sent ten strong men
to bring the Princess down.

In those days
a king's word was law.
The vagabone knew this;
and, what's more, he knew
he must marry the Princess,
whether he liked it or no.

The vagabone had great height,
but he stooped so
that it shortened the length
    of him.
His hair was long,
and it fell, uncombed and matted,
about his shoulders.
His brogues were patched,
his hose were sadly worn,
and with his rags
he was the sorriest cut of a man
that a maid
ever laid her two eyes on.
When the Princess came,
she was dressed in a gown of gold,
with jewels hanging
from every thread of it,
and her cap was caught
with a jeweled brooch.
She looked as beautiful
as a May morning—
with a thundercloud
rising back of the hills;
and the vagabone held his breath
for a moment, watching her.
Then he pulled the King
gently by the arm.

"I'll not have a wife
that looks grander than myself.
If I marry your daughter,
I must marry her in rags—
the same as my own."

The King agreed 'twas a good idea
and sent for the worst dress of rags
in the whole countryside.

The rags were fetched,
the Princess dressed,
the priest brought,
and the two of them married;
and, though she cried
and she kicked
and she cuffed and she prayed,
she was the vagabone's wife
—hard and fast.

"Now take her,
and good luck with ye,"
said the King.
Then his eyes fell on the tongs
by the hearth.
"Here, take these along—
they may come in handy
on the road."

Out of the castle gate,
across the gardens,
and into the country beyond
went the Princess
and the vagabone.
The sky was blue over their heads,
and the air was full of spring;
each wee creature
that passed them on the road
seemed bursting with the joy of it.
There was naught but anger
in the Princess's heart, however;
and what was in the heart
of the vagabone
I cannot be telling.
This I know,
that he sang the "Song of the Wren"
as they went.

Often and often
the Princess turned back
on the road or sat down,
swearing she would go no farther;
and often and often did she feel
the weight of the tongs
across her shoulders that day.

At noon the two sat down
by the crossroads to rest.

"I am hungry," said the Princess;
"not a morsel of food
have I tasted this day.
Ye will go get me some."

"Not I, my dear," said the vagabone;
"ye will go beg for yourself."

"Never," said the Princess.

"Then ye'll go hungry,"
said the vagabone;
and that was all.
He lighted his pipe
and went to sleep with one eye open
and the tongs under him.

One, two, three hours passed,
and the sun hung low in the sky.
The Princess sat there
until hunger drove her to her feet.

She rose wearily
and stumbled to the road.
It might have been the sound
     of wheels
that had started her,
I cannot be telling;
but as she reached the road,
a great coach
drawn by six black horses
came galloping up.
The Princess made a sign
for it to stop;
though she was in rags,
yet she was still so beautiful
that the coachman
drew in the horses
and asked her
what she was wanting.

"I am near to starving," she said.
The tears started to her eyes,
while a new soft note
crept into her voice.
"Do ye think your master
could spare me a bit of food—
     or a shilling?"
and the hand that had been used
     to strike
went out for the first time to beg.

It was a prince who rode
in the coach,
and he heard her.
Reaching out a fine, big hamper
through the window,
he told her she was hearty welcome
to whatever she found in it,
along with his blessing.
But as she put up her arms
for it, just, she looked—
and saw that the prince
was none other than the fat suitor
whose face she had slapped
on the day before.
Then anger came back to her
for the shame of begging from him.
She emptied the hamper—
chicken pasty, jam, currant bread,
and all—on top of his head,
and threw the empty basket
at the coachman.
Away drove the coach;
away ran the Princess
and threw herself, sobbing,
on the ground near the vagabone.

" 'Twas a good dinner that ye lost,"
said the vagabone; and that was all.

That night they reached
a wee scrap of a cabin
on the side of a hill.
The vagabone climbed the steps
and opened the door, saying,
"Here we are at home, my dear."

"What kind of a home
do ye call this?"
and the Princess stamped her foot.
"Faith, I'll not live in it."

"Then ye can live outside;
it's all the same to me."
The vagabone went in
and closed the door after him;
and in a moment
he was whistling merrily
the song of the wee brown wren.

The Princess sat on the ground
and nursed her poor tired knees.
She had walked many a mile
that day, with a heavy heart
and an empty stomach—
two of the worst
        traveling companions
ye can find.
The night came down,
black as a raven's wing;
the dew fell, heavy as rain,
wetting the rags
and chilling the Princess
to the marrow.

The wind blew fresh from the sea,
and the wolves began their howling
in the woods nearby;
and at last,
what with the cold and the fear
and the loneliness of it,
she could bear it no longer,
and she crept softly up
to the cabin and went in.

"There's the creepy-stool by the fire,
waiting for ye," said the vagabone;
and that was all.
But late in the night
he lifted her from the chimney corner
where she had dropped asleep
and laid her gently on the bed,
which was freshly made and clean.
And he sat by the hearth till dawn,
keeping the turf piled high
on the fire, so that cold
would not waken her.
Once he left the hearth;
coming to the bedside,
he stood a moment to watch her
while she slept,
and he stooped and kissed
the wee pink palm of her hand
that lay there
like a half-closed lough lily.

Next morning
the first thing
the Princess asked,
"Where is my breakfast?
Where are the servants?
Where are some decent clothes to put on?"

"Your servants are your own two hands,
and they will serve ye well
when ye teach them how,"
was the answer she got.

"I'll have neither breakfast nor clothes
if I have to be getting them myself.
And shame on ye for treating a wife so,"
and the Princess caught up a piggin
and threw it at the vagabone.

He jumped clear of it,
and it struck the wall behind him.
"Have your own way, my dear,"
and he left her
to go out on the bogs and cut turf.

That night the Princess hung the kettle
and made stir-about and griddle bread
for the two of them.

"'Tis the best I have tasted since I was a lad
and my mother made the baking," said the vagabone,
and that was all. But often and often his lips touched
the braids of her hair as she passed him in the dark;
and again he sat through the night, keeping the fire
and mending her wee leather brogues, that they might be whole
against the morrow.

Next day he brought some sally twigs and showed her
how to weave them into creels to sell on coming market day.
But the twigs cut her fingers until they bled,
and the Princess cried, making the vagabone white with rage.
Never had she seen such a rage in another creature.
He threw the sally twigs about the cabin,
making them whirl and eddy like leaves before an autumn wind;
he stamped upon the half-made creel, crushing it to pulp under his feet;
and, catching up the table, he tore it to splinters,
throwing the fragments into the fire, where they blazed.

"By Saint Patrick, 'tis a bad bargain that ye are!
        I will take ye this day to the castle in the next county,
                where I hear they are needing a scullery-maid;
                        and there I'll apprentice ye
                            to the King's cook."

"I will not go," said the Princess;
        but even as she spoke,
        fear showed in her eyes
        and her knees began shaking
            in under her.

"Aye, but ye will, my dear,"
        and the vagabone
        took up the tongs
            quietly
        from the hearth.

For a month the Princess worked
in the castle of the King,
and all that time
she never saw the vagabone.
Often and often
she said to herself, fiercely,
that she was well rid of him;
but often, as she sat alone
in the cool of the night,
she would wish for the song
of the wee brown wren,
while a new loneliness
crept deeper and deeper
into her heart.

She worked hard about the kitchen,
and she scrubbed the pots
and turned the spit
and cleaned the floor
with fresh white sand,
she listened to the wonderful tales
the other servants had to tell
of the King.

They had it
that he was the handsomest,
aye, and the strongest,
king in all of Ireland;
and every man and child
and little creature in his kingdom
worshiped him.
And after the tales were told,
the Princess would say to herself:
"If I had not been
so proud and free with my tongue,
I might have married such a king
and ruled his kingdom with him,
learning kindness."

Now it happened one day
that the Princess was told
to be unusually spry
and careful about her work;
and there was
a monstrous deal of it to be done:

cakes to be iced
and puddings to be boiled,
fat ducks to be roasted,
and a whole suckling pig
put on the spit to turn.

"What's the meaning of all this?"
asked the Princess.

"Ochone, ye poor
feeble-minded girl!"
and the cook looked at her
    pityingly.
"Haven't ye heard
the King is to be married this day
to the fairest princess
in seven counties?"

"Once that was I,"
thought the Princess,
and she sighed.

"What makes ye sigh?"
asked the cook.

"I was wishing, just,
that I could be having a peep
at her and the King."

"Faith, that's possible.
Do your work well,
and maybe I can put ye
where ye can see
without being seen."

So it came about,
as I am telling ye,
at the end of the day

when the feast was ready
    and the guests come,
that the Princess was hidden
behind the broidered curtains
in the great hall.
There,
where no one could see her,
she watched
the hundreds upon hundreds
of fair ladies and fine noblemen
in their silken dresses
    and shining coats
all silver and gold
march back and forth
across the hall,
laughing and talking
and making merry
among themselves.
Then the pipers began to play,
and everybody was still.
From the farthest end of the hall
came two and twenty lads
in white and gold;
and these were followed
by two and twenty pipers
in green and gold
and two and twenty bowmen
in saffron and gold
and, last of all, the King.

A scream, a wee wisp of a cry,
broke from the Princess,
and she would have fallen
had she not caught
one of the curtains.

For the King was as tall
and strong and beautiful
as Nuada of the Silver Hand;
and from the top
of his curling black hair
down the seven feet of him
to the golden clasps of his shoes,
he was every whit as handsome
as he had been that day
when she had cuffed him
in her father's castle.

The King heard the cry
and stopped the pipers.
"I think," said he,
"there's a scullery-maid
behind the curtains.
Someone fetch her to me."

A hundred hands
pulled the Princess out;
a hundred more pushed her
across the hall
to the feet of the King,
and held her there,
fearing lest she escape.
"What were ye doing there?"
the King asked.

"Looking at ye
and wishing I had the undoing
of things I have done,"
and the Princess hung her head
and sobbed piteously.

"Nay, sweetheart,
things are best as they are,"
and there came a look

into the King's eyes
that blinded those watching,
so that they turned away
and left the two alone.

"Heart of mine," he went on, softly,
"are ye not knowing me?"

"Ye are putting more shame on me
because of my evil tongue
and the blow my hand gave ye
        that day."

"I' faith, it is not so.
Look at me."

Slowly the eyes of the Princess
looked into the eyes of the King.
For a moment
she could not be reading them;
she was as a child
who pores over a strange tale
after the light fades
and it has grown too dark to see.
But bit by bit
the meaning of it came to her,
and her heart grew glad
with the wonder of it.
Out went her arms to him
with the cry of loneliness
that had been hers so long.

"I never dreamed that it was ye,
never once."

"Can ye ever love and forgive?"
asked the King.

"Hush ye!" and the Princess
laid her finger on his lips.

The tirewomen were called,
and she was led away.
Her rags were changed
for a dress
that was spun from gold
and woven with pearls,
and her beauty shone about her
like a great light.
They were married again that night,
for none of the guests were knowing
of that first
wedding
long
ago.

Late o' that night a singing *sthronshuch* came under the Princess's window, and very softly the words of his song came to her:

> *"The gay young wren sang over the moor.*
> *'I'll build me a nest,' sang he.*
> *' 'Twill have a thatch and a wee latched door,*
> *For the wind blows cold from the sea.*
> *And I'll let no one but my true love in,*
> *For she is the mate for me,'*
> *Sang the gay young wren.*
>
> *The wee brown wren by the hedgerow cried,*
> *'I'll wait for him here,' cried she.*
> *'For the way is far and the world is wide,*
> *And he might miss the way to me.*
> *Long is the time when the heart is shut,*
> *But I'll open to none save he,'*
> *Sang the wee brown wren."*

The grating opened slowly; the Princess leaned far out, her eyes like stars in the night, and when she spoke, there was naught but gentleness and love in her voice.

"Here is the silver I would have thrown ye on a day long gone by. Shall I throw it now, or will ye come for it?"

And that was how a princess of Connaught was won by a king who was a vagabone.

choral reading

Effective choral reading results from an earnest attempt
to follow the guidelines that tell how the poem is to be read.
These guidelines may be written by the author,
if he intends from the beginning that his poem is to be a choral reading
and therefore wants you to know how he wants the lines to sound.
They may also be written by another person who has interesting ideas
for arranging the author's selection as a choral reading.
They may even be written by your class,
after you have studied and experimented with a selection
and know how you want it to sound.
The important thing is — once the guidelines are written, follow them.

Some of the guidelines that follow in the choral reading
Our Country 'Tis of Thee ask you to chant,
to read proudly with full tones, to shout,
to slow down the reading, to read faster, and so on.
Once you are completely familiar with the poetry
and can read it like an "old friend,"
you will find it challenging to follow the author's directions
for interpreting the poetry.
Sometimes the directions call for *Voice 1, Voice 2, Narrator* or *A Woman.*
This simply means that a single person is to read a part.

If you plan to present *Our Country 'Tis of Thee* as a program,
remember that you don't have to memorize the parts.
Reading aloud from your books is a very acceptable way
for giving a choral reading program.

An essay by Bill Martin, Jr.

OUR COUNTRY 'TIS OF THEE

An historical cantata,
narration written by Ruth Roberts,
lyrics by Ruth Roberts and William Katz

All: We sing of thee, America,
Land we love, America,
Hear our song of Liberty,
Our country 'tis of thee.

Narrator: Our country 'tis of thee we sing,
land of New England meadows and southern cottonfields,
of county fairs, and ticker-tape parades,
barefoot boys with fishing rods
and Ladies' Day at the baseball park.
   A land of steel,
and industry,
and invention
with a heart as big as Texas
and dreams as tall as the great Northwest.

All: But where did it all begin?
Who made it possible?

Narrator: Well, to start with
There was a man...

260

There Was a Man

Narrator: John Smith, THERE WAS A MAN!

All: Hi, ho, diddle-i-o.

Narrator: Down in Jamestown he began . . . to make our country grow.

All: Make our country grow.

Narrator: Roger Williams, THERE WAS A MAN!

All: Hi, ho, diddle-i-o.

Narrator: In Rhode Island he began to make our country grow.

All: Make our country grow.

Narrator: Daniel Boone!

All: THERE WAS A MAN!

Narrator: Sam Houston!

All: THERE WAS A MAN!

Narrator: Brigham Young!

All: THERE WAS A MAN!

Narrator: Up in Utah he began to make our country grow.

All: Make our country grow.
Hi, ho, diddle-i-o.
That's the way that it all began.

Narrator: You can take my word for it.

All: Yes, you can!
Whenever there was a job to do,

Narrator: there was someone who

All: was a man!

Chanted joyously and rhythmically

Slowing the tempo

Spoken slowly but forcefully

Landing of the Pilgrims   A painting by Jack Hearne

Narrator: Where man goes, he carries his dreams with him.
And with the early settlers,
across three thousand miles of lonely ocean,
came the dreams of Freedom.
Its seeds were planted in Jamestown,
took root at Plymouth Rock, and —
as colonies spread up and down the Eastern seaboard —
the dream traveled
by horseback, by stagecoach, by foot,
by flatboats going up river . . .

Woman 1: It traveled to quiltin' parties . . .

Woman 2:   Sewin' bees . . .

Man: Town meetin's . . .

Boy: One-room schoolhouses . . .

262

Narrator: It traveled to Boston where they had a tea party —
to Virginia, where Patrick Henry made a fiery **speech** —
and finally, on July 4th, 1776,
the dream reached a hot, crowded Philadelphia **courthouse**.

*The scene shifts
to the Constitutional
Convention, 1776.*

All: *(Crowd noises, gavel knocking)*
Chairman: Order, gentlemen, please!
Sherman: *(Above crowd noises)* Mister Chairman!
Chairman: The Chair recognizes Roger Sherman, delegate **from Connecticut**.
Sherman: I move that the resolution
called "The Declaration of Independence"
be put to an immediate vote.
All: Yea! Hear! Hear!
Narrator: The thirteen colonies are going to take a vote!
There's the roll call beginning now!

263

Are You for Independence?

Chairman: Connecticut, ARE YOU FOR INDEPENDENCE?
Are you for the pursuit of happiness?
For life and liberty and freedom?

Solo 1: Connecticut votes yes!

Chairman: Rhode Island, ARE YOU FOR INDEPENDENCE?
Are you for the pursuit of happiness?
For life and liberty and freedom?

Solo 2: Rhode Island votes yes!

Chairman: Massachusetts, how 'bout you, sir?

Voice: Upon due reflection, we do, sir.

Chairman: Delaware and Pennsylvania?

2 Voices: Delaware and Pennsylvania vote yes!

Chairman: New York, New Hampshire and New Jersey?

3 Voices: The three of us vote yes!

Chairman: Virginia?

Solo: Virginia, home of Patrick Henry, George Washington,
Thomas Jefferson, James Madison and James Monroe
votes yes!

Chairman: Maryland and Georgia?

2 Voices: We agree, sir!

Chairman: North and South Carolina?

2 Voices: So do we, sir!

All: And that's how our country had its birthday,
a day that ev'rybody celebrates.
When thirteen original colonies became
The United States!

Independence Hall, Philadelphia   A painting by Robert J. Lee

Narrator: The voice of the people had spoken.
Liberty! Freedom!
The words thundered in a Revolutionary sky.
And Yankee Doodle America was ready to fight for them.
1781! A brand new nation had been born in revolution.
And now—slowly, painfully—we had to establish law and order,
settle our differences,
and, finally, frame a representative government.

Voice: Hey, Mister! We sure do have ourselves
a mighty fine Constitution.

Narrator: (*Proudly*) Nothing like it in the whole world!

Voice: But I was just wondering,
could you add a little something about Freedom?

Narrator: Can we? This is America. You bet we can!!
We'll put it all down on paper ...
the first ten amendments to the Constitution ...
and we'll call it *The Bill of Rights.*

That's What It Means to Be Free

All: You can say anything that you want to say
whoever you may be.
You can meet with your neighbors across the way.
THAT'S WHAT IT MEANS TO BE FREE.

*To be read
rhythmically
with strong accents,
not too slow*

You can write anything that you want to write
and dare to disagree.
You can sleep without feeling afraid at night.
THAT'S WHAT IT MEANS TO BE FREE.

You can't be imprisoned or taken away
until you've been justly tried.
You can choose the church where you want to pray
with your family by your side.

You can dream any dream that you want to dream
and make it all come true,
'cause you live in a land where the star of liberty
is shining over you.

Narrator: It took a lot of great men to keep
those stars of liberty shining ...
men like George Washington

*To be read
proudly
with full
tones*

Voice 1: ... Thomas Jefferson ...
Voice 2: ... Benjamin Franklin ...

Narrator: Great men!
But no story of America
could be told without the "Common Man"——
Mister Nobody-In-Particular——
whose restless eye and "itching foot"
led him West,
to change the nation's history.

266

All: . . . Step by step, mile by mile,
he coaxed his creaking wagon
through the ruts and rocks and mud
of the Wilderness Road

Voice 1: . . . through redskin arrows,

Voice 2: cholera epidemics,

Voice 3: and dried-up water holes

Narrator: . . . abandoning his favorite possessions along the way,
and burying the dead in unmarked graves
so the Indians wouldn't find them

Girls: . . . with nothing but prayer and will
to keep him going . . .

All: Goin' West in a covered wagon——
Git along, mule, giddiyap giddiyap
'Spite of the danger in Injun country
we're gonna cross
the Cumberland Gap.
Yes, we're gonna cross
the Cumberland Gap.

*To be chanted
like a fiddle tune*

Narrator: America was on its way
—linked to the vast unexplored West
by the Cumberland Gap,
doubled in size by the Louisiana Purchase.
We had little idea of where we were going,
but we were doggone determined to get there!

All: This was the pioneer American,
confident, daring, tough as an old hickory tree,
cutting through unbroken forests,
placing new trails across the mountains,
walking miles to the nearest schoolhouse.

Narrator: Working, singing, whoopin' and hollerin' his way
across an entire continent.

Boys: Clearin' the land,
cuttin' the timber,
storin' up sorghum, molasses and rye.
Puttin' down stakes,
raisin' up fences,
diggin' new wells when the water runs dry.

To be chanted with the rhythm and tempo of a square dance

Girls: (4) Ploughin', plantin',
rakin' and hoein',
workin' all day on the homestead site.
Churnin', weavin',
spinnin' and sewin',
until Saturday night.

All: With an empty jug
and a musical saw
we square dance to the
"Turkey in the Straw."
That's the way Maw got Paw.

Boys: Wagons ho!
Cross the Mississippi.
Here comes the stagecoach
bringin' us mail.

Girls: We're growin' up fast,
got a mill and an inn
and a church and a tavern
and a sheriff and a jail.

All: Over the plains
thru buffalo country;
Iowa, Kansas, Nebraska, too.
Fightin' off Injuns,
Pawnee, Shawnee,
Comanche, Apache,
Chippewa, Sioux.

Boys: Cowhands, cattlemen,
      headin' for Texas,
      pushin' their way
      thru the tall grassland.
      Fordin' the rivers,
      Arkansas, Cimarron,
      Brazos, Pecos,
      Rio Grande.

Girls: Hiyup to Oregon,
      'cross the Rockies,
      there where the pine trees grow so fine.
      Got traders, trappers,
      room to breathe,
      a respectable hotel,
      and a railroad line.

All: There's gold in the hills,
      silver in the canyons.
      Gotta move on thru drought and dust.
      Cow town, mining town,
      boom town, ghost town,
      Yipee-i-o!
      California or bust!

Slowly,
nostalgically

Thru many a mile
and many a moment,
many a man has left his mark.
Fremont, Hickok,
Buffalo Bill;
Kit Carson, Crockett,
Lewis and Clark.

Wagons Westward

A painting by William Reusswig

Narrator: Hey there, Mister, what's all the commotion about?
Man: Haven't you heard?
Abe Lincoln was elected President!
Narrator: Abraham Lincoln, sixteenth President of the United States—
a Kentucky-born, country lawyer,
who thirty years before
had split rails on the Sagamon River,
and whose neighbors named him "Honest Abe."
His election in 1860 set off an explosion
that had been building up for a half century.
Voice: The system of slavery is immoral.
It must not be extended to the new territories.
Voice 2: Cotton is King!
We need slave labor to grow cotton!

270

2 Voices:	The federal government must act....
2 Other voices:	The states have a right to decide for themselves!
More voices:	The states are a part of the Union...
Other voices:	*(Softly at first, then growing louder and louder)*

........Secession!

........the Union!

........Secession!

........the Union!

All: Secession! Secession! Secession!...Secession!

Unknown Bugle Boy of Cemetery Hill

All: There's a battlefield at Gettysburg
where swords and sabers rust
And brothers who were flesh and blood
are scattered in the dust.

*To be read
softly and
somewhat sadly*

But every night at Gettysburg
when everything is still,
They say a golden bugle blows
on Cemetery Hill.

Who was the unknown bugle boy
at Gettysburg that day
And was he wearing Yankee blue
or wearing Southern gray?

Voice: Why did he die? What was his motive?

*To be read
with
determination*

All: That government of the people, by the people,
and for the people shall not perish from the earth.

271

The Completion of the Transcontinental Railroad

The scene shifts to Utah.

Voice: We are gathered here at Promontory Point,
this historic day of May, 1869,
to witness the joining of two great railroads —
the Union Pacific from the East...

All: Hurray!

Voice: ...and the Central Pacific from the West...

All: Hurray!

Narrator: The last rail was laid, the last spike was driven,
and America had its first transcontinental railroad!
Other things were changing, too. Cities were rising,
factories were humming, industry was growing....

Voice 2: A four-wheel carriage run by an engine?
(Peals of laughter) Get yourself a horse!!!

Voice 3: A contraption that flies through the air
like a bird? *(More laughter)*
It'll never get off the ground!!!

Narrator: But there was no stopping a nation
of tinkerers and whittlers,
long accustomed to making,
repairing, improving and changing.
And with characteristic ingenuity and "git-up-and-go" —
America invented its way into the Industrial Age.

A picture by Betty Fraser

The Inventors' Song

All: It took Bell to make the telephone ring
AND it took Edison to light up our way
Oh, it took Robert Fulton in a steamboat
To go chug, chug, chuggin' down the bay.

Howe knew how to make a sewin' machine
The Wrights learned the right way to fly.
So when you're spellin' the word *America*,
don't forget to dot the *i* — for the Inventors —
Don't forget to dot the *i*.

George Pullman made the sleeping car for railroad trips at night.
Lew Waterman made the fountain pen so ev'ryone could write.
Richard Hoe made the rotary press so we could get the news.
Charles Goodyear made the rubber for the heels upon our shoes.

And when you talk about a new invention,
incidentally, don't forget to mention

that it took Morse to make the telegraph hum *(bee-de-beep)*,
Colt to make a Colt Forty-five *(bang-bang)*.
Oh, it took Henry Ford to make an auto *(toot toot)*,
So that folks could go and take a drive.

Otis made the elevator go up,
McCormick's reaper reaped the rye.
So when you're spelling the word *America*,
don't forget to dot the *i* — for the Inventors —
Don't forget to dot the *i*.

273

Narrator: Progress! That was the word that made the century turn.
Teddy Roosevelt setting a new style in politics,
women changing from hoop skirts to bloomers...
skyscrapers... ferris wheels... the moviola...
a bright new twentieth century of progress!

Man: Hold on, Mister. What about us human beings?
We could use a little of that progress, too.

Woman: He's right! This is nineteen hundred
and children are still working in factories.

All: We need progress! we need progress!

Voice 1: We got tenement houses and city slums!

Voice 2: A laboring man needs a living wage!

Voice 3: Constitution doesn't say that women can vote.

Voice 4: Me and my people — we want equality!

All: We need progress, progress! progress! progress!

Narrator: It was the beginning of a new interest
in human rights, in new freedom and liberty,
at home and in faraway places.

Voice 1: Dateline, Austria, 1914 —
GERMAN TROOPS HAVE CROSSED THE BORDER!

Voice 2: Dateline, Poland, 1915—WARSAW SURRENDERS!

Voice 3: Dateline, France, 1916—FRENCH ARMIES
ARE WEAKENING!

Shout the headlines.

Narrator: Dateline, America, 1917,

All: We *MUST* MAKE THE WORLD SAFE FOR DEMOCRACY!

Narrator: We had come to a decision! The World was our world,
and we were responsible for what went on in it.

The Whole Wide World Is My Home Town

All: I live on a street in my home town,
far away from a far-off land,
But THE WHOLE WIDE WORLD
IS MY HOME TOWN
when freedom needs a helpin' hand.

There's a peaceful sky in my backyard,
far away from fear and doubt,
But THE WHOLE WIDE WORLD
    IS MY HOME TOWN
and I've gotta help my neighbor out.

Narrator: Armistice Day, November 11, 1918.
We paraded and cheered, threw confetti,
and welcomed Johnny Doughboy home.
1919.

Boys: Jazz baby, where've you been?

Narrator: 1920.

Girls: Charleston! Charleston! Let's begin!

Narrator: 1921.

Voices: Stocks are going up.

Narrator: 1922.

Voices: I'm a flagpole sitter, how about you?

Narrator: 1923.

Voices: I'm a dapper flapper, boop-boop-a-doo.

Narrator: 1924.

Voices: I'll be down to get you in my new car, my new tin lizzie.

Narrator: 1925.

All: Stocks are going up.

Narrator: 1926.

Boys: Babe Ruth hit another home run this week.

Narrator: 1927.

All: Stocks are going up.

Narrator: 1928.

Girls: Well, I never would have bet
on a crystal radio set
you could even get Pittsburgh.

All: Stocks are going up, going up, going up, going up,
going up, up, up, up, up, up, up, up,   OH!!

The wild happiness breaks into despair on this word.

275

Narrator: The Stock Market crashed!...October, 1929.
We had mortgaged our homes, borrowed money,
danced to the tune of "get-rich-quick" —
and now we had to pay the piper.

Voice 1: If you mean the grocer, Mister, you're right!
We have no money to buy food!

Voice 2: No place to live, can't pay the rent.

Voice 3: No place to work. There aren't any jobs!

Narrator: The depression was the worst in the nation's history.
Ten million unemployed, bank failures, bread lines.

Voice: Brother, can you spare a dime?...

All: New Deal! New Deal!

Narrator: ...That was the promise of our newly elected President.
And while we watched anxiously, hopefully,
Franklin Delano Roosevelt rolled up his sleeves
and went to work!
The Roosevelt smile, his fireside chats,
his wife Eleanor and his little dog Falla...
these became part of the nation's memories.

There were other memories, too,
Pearl Harbor.... Guadalcanal.... D Day....

Girls: V for VICTORY.

Boys: An atom bomb that could shatter the world.

Narrator: A United Nations that could keep it together.

Boys: Give it to 'em, Harry!

Girls: President Harry S Truman!

Boys: We like Ike.

Girls: President Dwight D. Eisenhower!

Boys: All the way with J.F.K.

Girls: President John F. Kennedy!

*To be read
like, a political
slogan,
shouted
enthusiastically*

276

Voice: Countdown! *To be read like a rocket taking off*
All: Five, four, three, two, -oo . . . . . ONE!!! — der — ful.

Narrator: A wonderful new world of space, new frontiers, new vigor.
All: And suddenly . . . a new sorrow in the land.
Tears for a fallen President.
Muffled drums that whispered along the streets.
Narrator: But America goes on.

Voice: I, Lyndon B. Johnson, do solemnly swear that I will *To be read solemnly*
faithfully execute the office of President of the
United States, and will to the best of my ability,
preserve, protect, and defend the Constitution of
the United States. . . .

All: Yes, America goes on.
America will always go on and on.

My America

To be read with deep faith

All: Land I love, America,
Brave and free from shore to shore,
God be with you evermore.
Narrator: Let the word go forth,
from this time and place,
to friend and foe alike,
that the torch has been passed
to a new generation of Americans,
born in this century, tempered by war,
disciplined by a hard and bitter peace.
Proud of our ancient heritage. . . .

All: America, America,
God shed His Grace on thee,
And crowned thy good with brotherhood
from sea to shining sea.

THE END

creative dramatics

An essay by Bill Martin, Jr.,
picture by Kelly Oechsli

You probably have done creative dramatics
ever since you were in first grade:
sometimes you probably took turns reading
the conversation of several characters in a story;
other times you may have improvised a stage
and presented a "make-believe" story
with the simplest costumes and scenery;
and surely, at one time or another, you have given
a full-scale production with costumes, scenery, sound effects,
lighting—and, of course, an announcer.
Each of these excursions into creative dramatics
is worthwhile and has a definite place in the classroom.

The one danger to guard against
is that every play has to be a finished production.
That would be missing the fun
of acting out spontaneously any idea or story
that happens to strike your fancy.
You may be wondering how to make a play
out of a story like the Indian legend, "Piasa,"
in which very little conversation is given
and much is left to the imagination.
The first step is to read the story until you know it well.
Then make an outline of the story, listing each episode.
Then discuss each episode, figuring out how you can pantomime
the main action so that the play is interesting to see
as well as to hear.

After you have figured out the action for each episode,
then add speech to the action, letting each character
say naturally what he thinks is important to the situation.
For example, in the first episode when the Piasa
attacks the Indians on the river,
you may decide that nothing should be said
other than for the two Indians to scream, "The Piasa!
The Piasa! Save me from the Piasa!"
Of course, there are many other things that they might say
if you choose to give more details to the story in the first scene.
One of the best things you can do in getting a play off to a good start
is to make the first scene active and to present "the problem"
that needs solving.
In this case, it's how to get rid of the man-eating Piasa.
Even though there aren't many speaking parts in "Piasa,"
there is plenty of need for Indians, for water moccasin snakes,
for chanters in the background who also beat tom-toms,
and for people carrying signs to show the scene of action.
Also, there is need for many boys and girls
to link together to form the huge Piasa monster
that flies its way clumsily across the stage,
making its own horrifying noise.
With just this much discussion of "Piasa,"
perhaps you would like to leaf through this book
to find other stories and poems that lend themselves
to acting out.

Piasa

A legend adapted by Bill Martin, Jr.,
illustrated by Robert Shore

A strange
and horrible creature
once lived along the banks
of the Mississippi River near Alton, Illinois.
The monster was said to be
half bird and half dragon.
Its body was covered with green scales,
and its wings were those of a giant eagle.
The Indians called the creature
Piasa,[1] meaning "bird that devours men."

According to the legend, two young braves were attacked
by the Piasa one summer morning.
They had paddled out on the river at daybreak,
when, suddenly, the Piasa came flying toward them,
shooting flames from its mouth   [1] pronounced PIE-uh-saw
and screaming a cry that filled them with terror.
One Indian dived underwater and escaped,
but the other remained in the canoe, too frightened to move.
The Piasa grasped him in its sharp claws
and carried him up the river to its cave to devour him.

By noon of that day, the tragic news had penetrated[2]
the entire Illini[3] tribe, and a crowd of Indians
had surrounded Owatoga's[4] tent,
asking their beloved chieftain   [2] spread throughout
to save them from the Piasa.   [3] pronounced ih-LIE-nie
                                       [4] pronounced oh-wah-TOH-ga

For five days and nights
Owatoga fasted and prayed, asking the Great Spirit
to deliver his people from the danger of the Piasa.
During the fifth night, Owatoga's prayers were answered.
The Great Spirit spoke in a dream
and told how the Piasa could be destroyed.

281

Before daybreak
of the sixth morning,
Owatoga commanded six
of his finest braves
to follow him
to the top of a limestone cliff
overlooking the Mississippi River.

The braves carried
their strongest bows.
Their quivers were filled
with arrows that had been dipped
in poison milked from the mouths
of deadly moccasin snakes.

The braves threaded their bows
and hid behind huge rocks
at the top of the cliff.
Only old Owatoga was visible.
He stood on the edge of the cliff
overlooking the Mississippi River
waiting for the Piasa to come.

His wait was not long.
At dawn the Piasa came
from its cave
and flew noisily
up and down the river
looking for food.
When the monster saw Old Owatoga
standing on the edge of the cliff,
it screamed furiously
and dived toward him.

Old Owatoga dropped to the ground,
wrapping his arms around the roots
of a tree that grew out of the rocks.

The Piasa ripped and tugged
at Owatoga,
trying to pull him loose
from the tree,
but the old chieftain hung on
with superhuman strength.
At last the pain became too great,
and Old Owatoga
fell into unconsciousness.
He slumped limp on the ground
as if dead.

The Piasa screamed
a cry of victory
as it grasped the old man
in its claws
and raised its wings to fly away.

At that moment the Indian braves,
hidden behind the rocks,
shot at the beast.
Zing . . . zing . . . zing, zing . . . zing.
The poison arrows flew
straight to the mark,
hitting the monster
in the tender flesh
on the underside of its wings.

The monster screamed madly
and scrambled toward them
with eyes burning red
and fire shooting from its mouth.
But then the poison arrows
began to have effect.

283

The Piasa suddenly twisted
and writhed in agony.
Its screams could be heard
for ten miles
up and down the river.

Dropping Old Owatoga,
the Piasa clawed its way
to the edge of the cliff,
flapping its wings feebly.
Then, with one last effort,
it leaped into the air
and dropped into the maelstrom[5]
of the Mississippi River
one hundred feet below.
It was never seen again.

When the Indian braves were certain
that the Piasa was dead,
they carried their old chieftain
back to the village,
where the medicine men
cared for his wounds.

After he had recovered,
a great celebration was held.
The Illini Indians feasted and
danced for three days and nights
in honor of their chieftain
who had saved them
from the Piasa.

[5] pronounced MALE-strum; a
dangerous, swirling whirl-
pool.

On the fourth day
of the celebration,
the artists in the tribe
mixed their richest dyes
and went forth to the cliff
where the Piasa had been killed.
On the face of that cliff,
overlooking the Mississippi River
near Alton, Illinois,
the Indians painted
in flaming colors
a picture of the Piasa,
more than thirty feet high.

For a hundred years thereafter,
travelers going
up or down the Mississippi River
saw the life-size picture
of the Piasa
on the face of the white cliff,
and it became the custom
that every passing Indian
threaded his bow and shot an arrow
at the picture
of the man-eating monster.

In recent years,
a huge pile of broken arrows
was found at the base of the cliff.
Farther up the river,
a cave was found
in which were dried
and strewn bones
of many Indians.
Was this, then,
the home
of the Piasa monster?

Was there ever such a creature?
No, the Piasa never existed
except in the stories
of the Illini Indians.

Race

Wet wind, dark wind pushing through the trees,
Tall grass, cold grass, quick against my knees,
Wild night, black night, catch me if you can!
And I dashed down the hillside, and ran, and ran,
  and ran.

But the trees bent fiercely after,
And the long wind blew,
And the clouds piled faster, faster,
And the sharp grass grew,
And I stumbled through the hollows
As I raced, the panting night
Close at my heels,
Till we crashed into the light,
And I leaped up the stairs,
Two steps at a stride,
And banged the door behind me,
Safe inside.

A poem by Millicent Vincent Ward

Windy Nights

Whenever the moon and stars are set,
   Whenever the wind is high,
All night long in the dark and wet,
   A man goes riding by.
Late in the night when the fires are out,
   Why does he gallop and gallop about?

Whenever the trees are crying aloud,
   And ships are tossed at sea,
By, on the highway, low and loud,
   By at the gallop, goes he;
By at the gallop he goes, and then,
   By he comes back at the gallop again.

A poem by Robert Louis Stevenson.

Illustration by George Buckett

PROUD PEACOCK

Written and illustrated by Joseph Domjan

nce on a time, so long ago that it's almost forgotten, there was a poor young woodcutter who went deep into the forest each day to cut wood. It happened on the first day of spring that a little green snake fell in the way of the woodcutter's axe, and the woodcutter prepared to kill him.

"Pray, do not kill me," said the snake. "Spare my life, and I will give you any treasure that you desire. I am the king of the underground."

The woodcutter looked closely and saw a tiny gold crown on the little snake's head.

"I promise you diamonds or rubies or emeralds," said the snake. "You may choose gold or silver or platinum. Withhold your axe, and I will well fill your pockets."

"Little snake, what need have I of wealth?" said the woodcutter. "I am a lonely man, never hearing a voice but my own. I will spare your life if you will teach me to speak the language of the birds and animals. That would be wealth far greater than gold."

"Indeed, woodcutter," said the little snake, "you are a wise man."

The little green snake was a clever teacher, and the woodcutter was an eager pupil, and soon he could talk the language of the creatures living in the forest.

One morning a magpie called to him from a treetop, "Woodcutter! Woodcutter! Have you heard the news? The King has lost his favorite ring! Whoever finds it may have any treasure that the King possesses."

"All the people in the kingdom have gone to Buda to help in the search for the ring," said a bumblebee. "Everyone is off to help the King, the poor King."

"And you must go, too!" cried a butterfly. "You must leave the forest at once for Buda!"

"But I am only a poor woodcutter," said the young man. "The King would not welcome one such as I."

"Indeed, you are not rich," said a big black bear, "but you have wealth greater than gold. Who knows but your gift of language may help you serve the King?"

"Then, so be it," said the woodcutter. "I will leave at once to offer my services to the King."

So the woodcutter put a loaf of bread in one pocket and a square of cheese in the other, and set out for Buda.

The news of the King's misfortune traveled quickly, but his promise of a precious reward traveled faster. People throughout the land, all intent on collecting the reward, set out upon the main road leading to the palace, the woodcutter, among them, listening to their laughter and their dreams and to their complaints, of which there were many. From morning until night, he listened, he himself saying little, and the long, hard days of traveling passed quickly. At last he came to Buda.

There on a green hill stood the magnificent white palace of the King. It gleamed in the sunlight like snow on a mountain peak. The woodcutter had never seen such beauty. He entered the golden gates cautiously and stood aside to behold the garden. The courtyard was a flowering carpet laced with wax-leafed trees and

exotic shrubs from faraway countries. Schools of goldfish swam daintily in marble pools, and strange, brightly colored birds adorned the golden cages hanging from the boughs of trees. But the most dazzling sight of all was a proud peacock that strutted around a garden pool, admiring the reflection of his fiery tail in the water.

"Good morning, peacock," said the woodcutter. "I know every bird in the forest, but none is so handsome as you."

"True!" squawked the peacock. "I am a treasure . . . of the King," the peacock croaked.

"Surely a peacock has a sweeter voice to match his splendor," said the woodcutter.

"What's wrong with my . . . voice?" squawked the peacock. "Be gone, peasant, or I'll . . . *squawk!* . . . peck your eyes from your head!"

The woodcutter turned up the garden path to escape the angry peacock. At length, he entered the palace. The palace was a blaze of excited voices. Princes, knights, magicians and scholars ran about in handsome robes, screaming that the King had lost his ring. Pages, stable boys, chambermaids and butcher boys danced first on one foot, then on the other, crying, "I'll find it! Surely I'll find it!"

Old men, young men, pretty girls and otherwise, pushed and pulled and nudged one another as they crawled about on hands and knees, looking for the ring and thinking of the reward the King had offered for its return. The woodcutter edged his way through the confusion and bowed low to the King, and then to the Princess who sat at his side.

"Look! A ragamuffin!" said a courtier.

"A vagabond, and worse for it!" said another.

It suddenly became silent in the great hall as everyone stared at the poor woodcutter.

"Your Majesty," said the woodcutter, "I have found your ring."

"Yes?" said the King, doubtfully.

"Sire," said the woodcutter, "there is a proud peacock that stands by the garden pool."

"And well he might be proud!" said the Princess haughtily. "That peacock eats from my father's very own hand."

"Sire," said the woodcutter, ignoring the Princess's remarks, "the peacock has swallowed your ring."

"Have you been talking to the peacock?" asked the Princess, more haughtily than before.

"Indeed, your Majesty," said the woodcutter. "I have learned to talk with birds and animals. I know by the sound of the peacock's voice that something is lodged in his throat."

The whole court burst into laughter.

"And why," said the King, "do you think it is my ring that is lodged in the peacock's throat, and not a pebble?"

"Because," said the woodcutter, "the peacock is much too proud to eat a pebble. He would prefer a ruby."

"Father, dismiss this peasant," the Princess demanded. "We have heard enough of his foolishness."

The King stroked his beard thoughtfully. "No, let us pursue the woodcutter's notion. He may be a clever man. Fetch the peacock, and we shall see."

Twenty page boys ran to the garden and soon returned with the peacock, which they placed before the King. The peacock raised his head haughtily and spread his fiery tail with arrogant pride.

Suddenly the woodcutter grabbed the peacock and turned him upside down, shaking the peacock fiercely. Oh, how he shook him!

"Squawk!" cried the peacock. "Squawk! Squawk!"

"Give up the ring," said the woodcutter, firmly.

"I won't!" cried the peacock. "*Squawk, squawk!*"

"Fool!" screamed the Princess. "You are hurting the peacock! Let him go, this instant!"

The woodcutter shook the peacock again; oh, how he shook him! "Squawk! Squawk!"

Clink! The ring fell from the peacock's throat and rolled across the marble floor.

The embarrassed peacock slunk from the room, and the Princess fled after him.

"My ring! My beautiful ring!" cried the King. "Woodcutter, you have found my lost treasure!"

Everyone in the palace crowded closer to see. "Oh, look! The King has found his ring! Long live the King! He has found his favorite ring!"

The King slipped the ring on his finger. "Come, my friend," he said to the woodcutter. "You are to be my guest at dinner. You are a clever man, indeed."

The woodcutter was seated to the right of the King at a long marble table. The Princess neither looked at him nor spoke to him as she paraded into the hall with jewels shimmering on every thread of her satin dress. Lords and ladies followed, taking their places at the table according to their rank. And so the dinner began.

The food was served on golden plates, and the wine was poured into golden goblets. It kept coming from the royal kitchen, platter after platter full, each dish more tempting than the last. The poor woodcutter had never seen such grandeur nor so much food, but he was so hungry that he ate heartily.

When the dinner was over, the King began, "My friend, you may have any treasure that I possess, except, of course, my favorite ring."

The woodcutter looked about. Before him lay bowls of white glass inlaid with silver and turquoise, delicate roses made of gold and adorned with pearls and rubies, carpets loomed with costly yarns in faraway places, handsomely carved chairs upholstered with silver brocade.

"Sire, of all your treasures," said the woodcutter, "I choose her." He pointed to a Princess who sat across and down the table from him.

"Impossible!" said the Princess, staring angrily at the woodcutter. "I am not a piece of chattel to be auctioned off at a country fair!"

"She is the dearest treasure in the palace," said the woodcutter. "I choose her."

"This is a bit upsetting," said the King. "I hadn't thought of your choosing the Princess."

"Then, Sire," said the woodcutter, "you haven't been a poor woodcutter living deep in the forest where one seldom hears a human voice."

"Nonsense!" screamed the Princess. "I shan't be given like a hunting dog!"

"Her voice doesn't match her beauty at all," said the woodcutter, "but I have chosen a treasure nonetheless."

"My dear fellow," said the King, drawing the woodcutter aside, "you're making a grave error! The Princess is terribly haughty and utterly useless. She needs a sound spanking; but, of course, no one ever spanks a Princess."

"Come, fairest Princess," said the determined woodcutter. "Let us be wed so we can get back to my work in the forest."

"I won't," screamed the Princess.

"Aye, you will," said the woodcutter. He grabbed the Princess, turned her upside down, and shook her.

"Stop!" she screamed. "Stop! Stop!"

"I'll stop, indeed," said the woodcutter, "when you are ready for our wedding."

The woodcutter shook the Princess again; oh, how he shook her!

"Stop!" cried the Princess. "Set me down, this instant!"

At last the Princess was so shaken that she said weakly, "Let the wedding begin."

The palace was in an uproar.

"Woodcutter, think twice," said the King. "It will be much more difficult to teach the Princess to cook than it was to find a ring."

"Indeed, it will," said the woodcutter, "but she will learn."

"You are a determined man," said the King, "but you have, I think, an impossible task before you. If you succeed in teaching the Princess to work," the King chuckled at the prospects—"I will give you half of my kingdom."

"Then let the wedding begin," said the woodcutter. "I have much work to do."

And so the woodcutter and the Princess were married, and he took her home in a donkey cart.

The next morning the woodcutter awakened early, but not the Princess. She remained in bed, pretending to be asleep.

"It's time to get up, my dear," said the woodcutter firmly. "I said it is time to get up."

When the Princess failed to stir, the woodcutter picked her up bodily and set her on her feet.

"Fool!" she screamed. "I refuse to get up! I am a Princess, not a kitchen maid."

"Indeed, you are a Princess," said the woodcutter, "but you are also my wife. Today, while I am at work, I want you to make the bed, light the fire, cook the food, sew my shirts, and clean the cottage. That will be a fair start at learning to be my wife." Then the woodcutter said good-by and set out to work, eager to tell the birds and animals of his good fortune.

When the woodcutter returned home that evening, the bed was not made, the fire was out, the food was not cooked, his shirts were not sewn, the cottage had not been cleaned, and, alas! the Princess was gone.

"Good woodcutter," said the wren that made its home under the eaves of the cottage, "the Princess is hiding in the haycock. She has been there all day."

"Thank you, friend wren," said the woodcutter. "I'll have her home in a hurry."

The woodcutter walked straight to the haycock and uncovered the Princess from her hiding place. She was admiring herself in a mirror.

"Woodcutter! Be mindful!" screamed the Princess. "A Princess mustn't be spanked."

"Indeed, I remember," said the woodcutter.

Before she could flee, the woodcutter caught the Princess, turning her, dress and all, over his knee. Then he gave her a spanking that all of the forest, and especially the Princess, would remember. *Whack! Whack! Whack! Whack! Whackety, whackety, whack!*

"Stop! Stop!" screamed the Princess. "You mustn't spank a Princess. My father, the King, said so."

" 'Tis not you I'm spanking, my dear," said the woodcutter. "It's your lazy dress I'm spanking."

Whack! Whack! Whack! Whackety, whackety, whack!

"No more! No more!" cried the Princess. "I've had enough!"

"Not quite enough!" said the woodcutter.

He gathered the Princess in his arms and he kissed her once, twice, and then three times. And once more he kissed her to dry her tears.

When he and the Princess returned to the cottage, she lighted the fire and quietly prepared their supper while the woodcutter rested in his chair and sang her love songs that had no endings.

When the woodcutter and his wife went back to the palace at Buda, the King could see that he had no treasure more precious than his obedient and beautiful daughter. Just as he had promised, the King gave the woodcutter half of his kingdom and all of his blessing.

And after all, the woodcutter deserved it, for as the magpie told the fiery peacocks that stood in the garden preening their feathers, the woodcutter *was* a very clever man, and he and his Princess were just the sort of people who should live happily forever.

Which is exactly what they did.

It's very interesting what happens to ordinary words
when they are used in ways that make us see and hear them
as if we had never encountered them before.
In "The Cataract of Lodore," the poet Robert Southey
uses very ordinary words to create the sound and the appearance
of rushing water.
Even when he uses a word that may be new to you,
he uses it in combinations of known words
that tell you how to pronounce it.
And isn't it interesting that his way of grouping the words
gives a picture of the speed and the strength and the depth
of the water as it comes down the mountain?

An essay by Bill Martin, Jr.

The Cataract of Lodore

An excerpt from a poem by Robert Southey

"How does the water
Come down at Lodore?"
My little boy asked me
Thus, once on a time;
And moreover he tasked me
To tell him in rhyme.
So I told him in rhyme,
For of rhymes I had store:

The cataract strong
Plunges along,
Striking and raging
As if a war waging
Its caverns and rocks among:
Rising and leaping,
Sinking and creeping,
Swelling and sweeping,
Showering and springing,
Flying and flinging,
Writhing and ringing,
Eddying and whisking,
Spouting and frisking,
Turning and twisting
Around and around
With endless rebound!
Smiting and fighting
A sight to delight in;
Confounding, astounding,
Dizzying and deafening
    the ear with its sound.

Collecting, projecting,
Receding and speeding,
And shocking and rocking,
And darting and parting,
And threading and spreading,
And whizzing and hissing,
And dripping and skipping,
And hitting and splitting,
And shining and twining,
And rattling and battling,
And shaking and quaking,
And pouring and roaring,
And waving and raving,
And tossing and crossing,
And running and stunning,
And flowing and going,
And foaming and roaming,
And dinning and spinning,
And dropping and hopping,
And working and jerking,
And guggling and struggling,
And heaving and cleaving,
And moaning and groaning;
And glittering and frittering,
And gathering and feathering,
And whitening and brightening,
And quivering and shivering,
And hurrying and skurrying,
And thundering and floundering;

Dividing and gliding and sliding,
And following and brawling and sprawling,
And driving and riving and striving,
And sprinkling and twinkling and wrinkling,
And sounding and bounding and rounding,
And bubbling and troubling and doubling,
And grumbling and rumbling and tumbling,
And clattering and battering and shattering,
Retreating and beating and meeting and sheeting,
Delaying and straying and playing and spraying,
Advancing and prancing and glancing and dancing,
Recoiling, turmoiling, and toiling and boiling,
And gleaming and streaming and steaming and beaming,
And rushing and flushing and brushing and gushing,
And flapping and rapping and clapping and slapping,
And curling and whirling and purling and twirling,
And thumping and plumping and bumping and jumping,
And dashing and flashing and splashing and clashing,
And so never ending, but always descending,
Sounds and motions for ever and ever are blending,
All at once and all o'er, with a mighty uproar,
And this way the water comes down at Lodore.

Wild Bugles of the Mountains

The wild bugle of the bull elk
is one of the most exciting sounds in the animal kingdom.
The elk's mating call starts very low
and keeps getting higher and higher,
until it is a piercing, whistlelike sound.
Many old-time mountaineers who should know
insist that the elk's call has a wider range of notes
from low to high than any other North American animal,
including the cougar with its bloodcurdling scream
and the now very rare timber wolf with its spine-tingling howl.

An essay by Bernard Martin,
illustrations by Bernard Martin

303

I'll never forget the first time
I heard a lovesick Wapiti
(a name the Shawnee Indians
and scientists
bestowed on the elk)
bugle his challenge
over an alpine[1] meadow.
I was high on a ridge
overlooking the Madison River
in Yellowstone National Park.
Suddenly, the thin September air
was rent by a mighty wail.
The sound started on a low note,
as though a banshee[2]
were wailing in the valley,
and rose steadily
until it ended
in a shrill, sirenlike scream
that stabbed my ears.

[1] mountain

[2] a wailing spirit that, according to Gaelic folklore, warned a family of approaching death

As the sound echoed
through the pines
and ricocheted[3]
off the towering mountain peaks,
the call ended with a series
of short deep grunts.
Then followed the whack of antlers
as the bull elk thrashed fiercely
at shrubs and saplings.

The sound was electrifying.
All life in the area
seemed to pause, listening.
In a few moments
an old herd bull
on a neighboring hill
bugled a reply
to the young challenger.

Actually, the elk's call
bears little resemblance
to the notes produced by a bugle.
The sound is more nearly
a rising whistle,
similar to one you might make
by blowing into a pop bottle,
easily at first,
then harder and harder.
In fact, many hunters lure bulls
into gun range
by blowing blasts on homemade
or manufactured whistles.

The bugling of the elk
is generally confined to the males.
Cows occasionally whistle,
but their call lacks the spirit
of the sound pumped from the lungs
of a lovesick bull.

[3] rebounded

But bugling is not confined
solely to mature animals.
Young bulls also whistle.
The bugle of an old patriarch[4]
sounds coarse and harsh.
The call of a six-to-
eight-year-old bull
is a blast of full, mellow notes.
A very young bull whistles
a series of thin squeaky notes
and, therefore, is called a *squealer*.
When a dozen bulls
of different ages
respond to the challenging whistle
of another bull,
the mountain "rings"
with the weird racket.

Elk calls are heard
only in the fall
during the mating season.
Throughout most of the year,
the animals lead a rather quiet
and orderly life.
But with the coming
of the mating season,
which usually starts
in late August
and continues until late October,
one of the most dramatic happenings
unfolds in the woodlands.

It is then
that the magnificent bull elk,
the largest and most handsome
member of the deer family,
tunes up his bugle
and goes forth
to gather his harem.
It is a time of challenging,
bugling and whistling.
It's a time of sparring
and practicing sham battles
on young trees and shrubs.

[4] the old leader of a herd

305

It's a time
when outrider bachelor bulls
prowl like bandits,
ready to race in and steal the cows
from a careless or less able bull.
It's a time of recklessness
and danger.
No bull will give up his cows
without a fight.
He may lose his life in doing so,
but he instinctively
protects his rights.

A big bull will often collect
a harem of twenty-five
or thirty cows.
If he is defeated by a challenger,
he loses his herd.

An old herd bull may fight
many savage do-or-die battles,
but he attempts to bluff his way
out of as many encounters
as possible.
Often a bull can rout an adversary
by making a charge so furious
that the challenger retreats
out of sheer fright.

A couple of Septembers ago,
I watched a tremendous bull
guard his harem by a big bluff
that saved him from actual combat.

I was in the low Shirley Mountains
of central Wyoming.
Bull elk were swaggering
around the hills,
trying to collect herds.
Their whistles and grunts filled the air.
I stood hidden,
watching an open meadow
surrounded by a thick stand
of pine trees.
Presently a mammoth bull
policed his harem of eighteen cows
into the opening.
He was a powerful animal.
I judged his height
to be five feet at the shoulders.
But he appeared over nine feet tall
because of a magnificent pair
of antlers.
There was no question about it,
this bull was the king
of the mountain.

Shortly after the harem
entered the meadow,
I spotted four outrider bulls
lurking in the trees.
They were waiting
for an opportunity to raid the cows.

Presently, one of the outriders
stretched his neck
and bugled a threat to the herd bull.
The old sultan ignored the call.
After a few minutes,
the outrider repeated his challenge
and swaggered closer to the herd.
His act of aggression
triggered the old bull into action.
He tossed his giant antlers,
stretched his neck
and blasted the air with a
*Whooooo-oooooooo-eeeeeeee-
UNH-UNH-UNH.*
Then lowering his head in rage,
he plowed the earth with his antlers
and tossed a cloud of dirt
high over his back.
Then he charged.

The intruder was so terrified
by this display
that he turned and fled.

But now the old bull
was in a great rage.
He turned
to the three other outriders nearby
and chased them off, too.
A few minutes later,
the wise old warrior
prodded his cows onward,
and the herd passed from my sight
as they moved
up the mountain slope.

By late October
the mating season
has run its course.
The bull elk are calm.
They quietly rejoin the herd
under the leadership
of the old patriarch,
or they form their own band
and go off.
The bugles of the mountain tops
will be muted for another year.

Little Oscar was at bat.
He shut his eyes
and swung at the ball.
And he hit it.
But it was
a very short hit.
He only got to first base.

"What is the score?"
Pieter shouted.

"The Indians are ahead,"
Father Denbooms
told him sadly.
"Two to one."

"Then we still have a chance,"
Pieter said.

"Yes,"
Father Denbooms said.
"The Indians were expecting
your fast pitching.
Little Oscar's slow pitches
fooled them for a while.
But it is the last
of the ninth inning.
We have two out,
and we must make
two runs to win."

"Give me a bat,"
Pieter shouted.
Then he sighed.
"If I only had
my good ash bat," he said.

How Baseball Began in Brooklyn
by LeGrand

He picked up
the bat
Oscar had used.
It gleamed like silk
in the sunlight.
Pieter looked at it
again,
and his nose wiggled
very fast.

"No!" Pieter said.
"It can't be.
This is my good ash bat!"
He shouted to Oscar,
"Oscar,
where did you find my bat?"

"Oh, I had it all the time,"
Oscar said.
"I hid it because I knew
you'd go and look for it.
That was the only way
I could get into the game.
And I knew you'd lose
without me."

"You!" Pieter shouted.
"You have lost the game for us.
You have ruined
the whole Denbooms family."

A story by LeGrand,
pictures by Bill O'Day

"I have not," Oscar said.
"I played good.
I am on first base.
If you hit the ball, we win."
Pieter swung his good ash bat
to get the feel of it.
It swished through the air
with a sound like a cheer.
But he missed.
Nine Feathers drew his arm back

and pitched.............

Pieter swung hard at the ball.

But he missed again.

"Two strikes,"
Chief Kakapateyuo shouted.
"One more strike and we win."

The other Indians all shouted,
"Beat Dembums. Beat Dembums."

Nine Feathers pitched again.
Pieter took a deep breath.
He gripped his bat hard.
He swung.
He hit the ball so hard
that his fingers tingled,
and the bat rang
like a whole chime of bells.

The ball soared

up over the trees. It went on and on. It was just a speck in the distance.

Little Oscar ran around the bases
and came in with another run,
and the Denbooms won the game,
three to two.

"That was the run
that saved our home,"
Father Denbooms shouted.
"It was the first time
anyone hit the ball so far
he could go around all the bases
and come back to home plate.
Truly a home run it was."

Little Oscar grinned happily.
"But don't forget I made a run,
too," he said.
"Our side would not have won
without me."

"Yes, you have won,"
Chief Kakapateyuo said.
"And I will keep my word.
Your farm is safe."

Then the chief said,
"But I am still angry
because you bought your land
with bad beads."

The chief held out his hands.
They were filled with the beads
Father Denbooms had given him.

"Why, Chief,"
  Father Denbooms said,
"those are fine beads.
  They are not broken.
  The color is bright."

"It is the color which is bad,"
  the chief said.
"The color of pink.
  My friend, Chief Manquen,
  has told me
  pink is the color for women.
  He laughs at me
  when I wear these beads."

  Father Denbooms thought about it.
  Then he said,
"Chief, I can exchange them
  for beads which are blue
  or red or green."

"Blue is a good color,"
  Kakapateyuo said.
"It is a color for a chief.
  Chief Manquen has beads
  which are blue."

"Blue beads you shall have,"
  Father Denbooms said.

  Chief Kakapateyuo smiled.
"Now I am not angry any longer,"
  he said.
  And he shook hands
  with Father Denbooms.

  While Father Denbooms
  and the chief were talking,
  Pieter crept into the woods.
  He was worried about the Indian
  who had been caught in the trap.

"A wildcat or a bear
might get him,"
Pieter told himself.

But when Pieter found the trap,
the Indian was not there.
He had broken the vine
and escaped.

"I am glad," Pieter said.
"He will not
make any more trouble for us.
He would not want
the other Indians to know
how he was caught in a trap."

	1	2	3	4	5	6	7	
Breukelen Denbooms	0	0	1	0	1	0	1	3
Canarsie Indians	0	1	0	1	0	0	0	2

Pieter went back
to the ball field.
Father Denbooms was building up
the Indians' old fire
back of first base.
Then he brought deer
from his smokehouse
and cooked it.
Mother Denbooms brought pickles
and pies and crullers and cheese.

The Denbooms and the Indians
had a feast together,
and they cheered the new game,
which they named Baseball.

"It is a wonderful game,"
said the chief.
"I say it,
and I am Kakapateyuo,
Chief of the Canarsies."

And everyone agreed with him.

And little Oscar ate more
than anyone at the feast.

And that is how
the Denbooms' farm was saved.
And that is how baseball
came to Brooklyn,
for after the Denbooms' farm
was safe, more Dutch people
came to Cow Cove.
When there were enough
people there to make a village,
they called it Breukelen,
after a town in Holland.
And when it became a city,
the name was changed
to Brooklyn.

But if Pieter Denbooms
had not invented baseball
and won that first game,
there would be no city
named Brooklyn today.

The Coin

Into my heart's treasury
  I slipped a coin
That time cannot take
  Nor a thief purloin,—
Oh, better than the minting
  Of a gold-crowned king
Is the safe-kept memory
  Of a lovely thing.

by Sara Teasdale

Spring

I'm shouting
I'm singing
I'm swinging through trees
I'm winging skyhigh
With the buzzing black bees.
I'm the sun
I'm the moon
I'm the dew on the rose.
I'm a rabbit
Whose habit
Is twitching his nose.
I'm lively
I'm lovely
I'm kicking my heels.
I'm crying "Come dance"
To the fresh water eels.
I'm racing through meadows
Without any coat
I'm a gamboling lamb
I'm a light leaping goat
I'm a bud
I'm a bloom
I'm a dove on the wing.
I'm running on rooftops
And welcoming spring!

by Karla Kuskin

Song: The Owl

When cats run home and light is come,
  And dew is cold upon the ground,
And the far-off stream is dumb,
  And the whirring sail goes round,
  And the whirring sail goes round;
Alone and warming his five wits,
The white owl in the belfry sits.

When merry milkmaids click the latch,
  And rarely smells the new-mown hay,
And the cock hath sung beneath the thatch
  Twice or thrice his roundelay,
  Twice or thrice his roundelay;
Alone and warming his five wits,
The white owl in the belfry sits.

by Alfred, Lord Tennyson,
drawing by Chet Reneson

317

GOING BEYOND READING

Sometimes your reading may leave you with more questions
than answers.

    1) This may have happened when you read "Space Ship Bifrost"
       and discovered that the story stopped
       just as the space flight began.

    2) Or, it may have happened when you read "Hopi Snake Dance"
       and found yourself wondering about other rituals
       involving snakes.

Your reading may also propel you into certain activities
that seem necessary before you feel satisfied with the reading.

    1) You may conduct research to satisfy your wondering.

    2) You may write a poem that began coming into your mind
       as you viewed a painting or read another author's poem.

    3) You may make a painting or drawing to express feelings
       that were stirred up by your reading.

Let's take a look at the poem "What Is Black?" on page 319.
After reading the poem, what are your reactions?
Do you agree with the author's notions of black
or do you have some more interesting notions of your own?
Is there some particular picture of black
that you would like to go back to and think about?

        The sound of black is
        "Boom! Boom! Boom!"
        Echoing in
        An empty room.

And how about red? or blue? or yellow?

An essay by Bill Martin, Jr.

Are you moved to do some creating of your own
after reading this poem? Might you write
your own poem? paint a picture? arrange a choral reading?

Reading serves one of its best purposes
when it arouses such feelings or creates such curiosity
that you want to carry the ideas and feelings further.
Which selections in *Sounds of a Distant Drum*
have had this kind of an effect on you?

What Is Black?

A poem by Mary O'Neill

Black is the night
When there isn't a star
And you can't tell by looking
Where you are.
Black is a pail of paving tar.
Black is jet
And things you'd like to forget.
Black is a smokestack
Black is a cat,
A leopard, a raven,
A high silk hat.
The sound of black is
"Boom! Boom! Boom!"
Echoing in
An empty room.
Black is kind—
It covers up
The run-down street,
The broken cup.
Black is charcoal
And patio grill,
The soot spots on
The window sill.
Black is a feeling
Hard to explain
Like suffering but
Without the pain.
Black is licorice
And patent leather shoes
Black is the print
In the news.
Black is beauty
In its deepest form,
The darkest cloud
In a thunderstorm.
Think of what starlight
And lamplight would lack
Diamonds and fireflies
If they couldn't lean against
Black.....

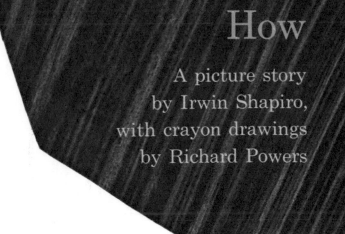

How

A picture story
by Irwin Shapiro,
with crayon drawings
by Richard Powers

The reason Old Stormalong is a big legendary hero
is that he was big to start with.
He was the toughest, strongest, screwiest, noisiest,
laughingest guy on the sea, on a ranch, and in a forest.
He bragged himself even bigger than he was,
and when his pals, buddies, and shipmates
repeated his brags, they made the big brags even bigger.
So when I started drawing Old Stormy,
he came out shouting up a tornado!
Sometimes he came on so strong that he took up
all of the room on the page;
sometimes he swelled up so big that he squeezed the words
into a corner and left me talking with colors!
But Irwin Shapiro's marvelous tale of Old Stormy
is all here, spread out as big as Stormy himself.
After all, there's no use arguing with a legend.

Richard Powers, the artist

Old Stormalong
captured
Mocha
Dick

There are many stories
about who captured Mocha Dick,
the Great White Whale,
or Moby Dick,
as he was sometimes called.
But any sailorman
worth his salt knows
that it was Old Stormalong—
and he had to become a cowboy
to do it.

Alfred Bulltop Stormalong
was the greatest sailor
who ever lived.

323

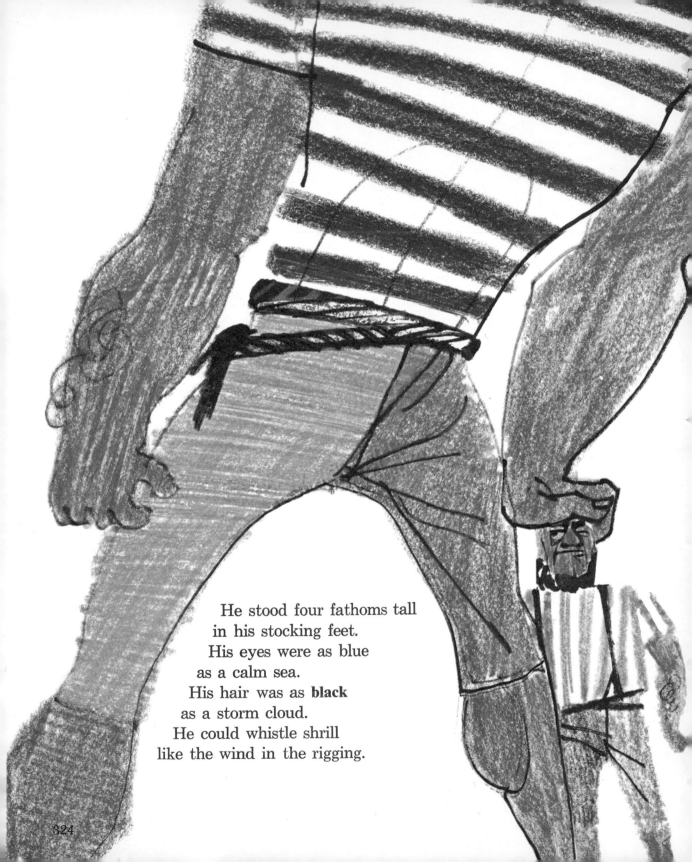

He stood four fathoms tall
in his stocking feet.
His eyes were as blue
as a calm sea.
His hair was as **black**
as a storm cloud.
He could whistle shrill
like the wind in the rigging.

He could hoot like a foghorn;
and he could talk ordinary,
just like anyone else.

Stormalong had one fault.
He was always complaining
that they didn't make ships
big enough for him.

One windy night
Stormalong was sitting
in the Sailors' Snug Haven,
the inn that served
the best shark soup
in the town of Nantucket.
He was sitting cross-legged
on the floor
so that his head
wouldn't bump
the ceiling.
He ate
six dozen oysters,
then called for some shark soup,
which he drank from a dory.

Beside him
sat Captain Joshua Skinner
of the good ship *Dolphin*
and some members of the crew.
Stormalong was to sail
with them the next morning
to catch whales
in the Pacific Ocean.

"Captain Skinner,"
said Stormalong
"on this voyage
I'm going to capture
Mocha Dick."

"Hm," said Captain Skinner.
"You've said that
five times before.
And five times
the white whale escaped you."

"This time he won't escape!"
shouted Stormalong,
hooting like a foghorn.
Then he added
in an ordinary voice,
"And I mean it, too."

"Hm," said Captain Skinner.
"You meant it
the other five times.
And still Mocha Dick
swims the seas."

"Aye, 'tis easy
to capture the white whale—
with words,"
said a little sailor
with red whiskers,
while all the other sailors laughed.

"Laugh while you may,"
said Stormalong angrily.
"You'll be singing
a different tune
when the *Dolphin* comes back
to port."

"If you are so sure of yourself,"
said the innkeeper,
"write it down here."
And he handed Stormalong
one of the slates
on which he kept accounts.

"Aye, that I will,"
said Stormalong.
Picking up the slate,
he wrote in big letters:

ON THIS VOYAGE OF THE
DOLPHIN
I WILL CAPTURE MOCHA
DICK
SIGNED ALFRED BULLTOP
STORMALONG

The innkeeper hung the slate up
over the fireplace for all to see.

"Aye, mateys!"
roared Stormalong.
"This time
Mocha Dick will meet his doom!"

Stormalong finished
his shark soup in one gulp.
Then he whistled shrill
like the wind in the rigging
and left the inn.

The next morning
a crowd of people
was at the dock
to say good-by
to the *Dolphin*'s brave crew.

"Good luck, lads!" they shouted.
"A short voyage
and a greasy one!
Fair winds, calm seas!
Beware of Mocha Dick!"

"Let Mocha Dick beware,
for Alfred Bulltop Stormalong
is out to capture him!"
said Stormalong,
hooting like a foghorn.

"Belay there!
Enough of your boasting!"
said Captain Skinner.
Then he turned to the first mate
and said, "Cast off!"

And a cheer went up
as the *Dolphin* caught the wind
in her sails
and went out to the open sea.

For nine months the *Dolphin*
sailed the Pacific Ocean.
Wherever she went,
there was always a lookout
in the crow's nest
high on the mast.
Every time the lookout
spied a whale, he would shout,

**"Blo-o-ows!
Thar she blows!"**

And the men would jump
into rowboats and give chase to the whale.

One day the lookout in the crow's nest called out,
"Blo-o-ows! Thar she blows! Whale off the port side!
Thar she blows and breaches! And Mocha Dick, at that!"

"Man the boats!" ordered the captain. "Lower away!"
The men set out over the side of the ship
in little boats and rowed toward Mocha Dick.
Stormalong stood in the stern of his boat,
waving his harpoon in the air.

"After him, me hearties!" he shouted. "Faster, lads, faster!
There he is now!"
And indeed they could see Mocha Dick's ugly face
rising out of the sea. With a rumble and a roar
the Great White Whale sent a spout of water
high into the air. He was almost as big as the *Dolphin*,
and he was the color of sea foam in the light of a misty moon.

As if to warn Stormalong, he opened his mouth
and showed his great sharp teeth.

"After him, mateys!"
cried Stormalong.
"A dead whale
or a stove boat!"

With a shout,
Stormalong let his harpoon fly
at Mocha Dick.
It stuck in the whale's back.
But Mocha Dick
just gave himself a shake
and began to swim away.
The harpoon was attached
to the boat by a long rope,
and as Mocha Dick swam along,
he pulled the boat after him.

"Hold fast, mates!"
said Stormalong.

S w o o s h ! And off they went
across the water.
Faster and faster
swam Mocha Dick,
with the little boat bobbing
and bouncing after him.
Soon they had left the *Dolphin*
far behind.

"Here we go on a sleigh ride!"

Suddenly Mocha Dick stopped. He heaved himself into the air,
and the rope broke with a snap. The harpoon remained
in his back, a little bit of rope flying from it
like a flag of victory. He dove below the water,
gave a flip of his tail, and the boat overturned.
With a splash, Stormalong and his mates tumbled into the sea.

"We are lost!"
cried one of the sailors.
"Mocha Dick is coming back!
He will swallow us all!"

But Mocha Dick just pushed his way
close to Stormalong and opened his mouth
in a big grin.

His body
shook
as though
he
were laughing.

Then
he spouted a stream of water
right into Stormalong's face,

grinned again,

and swam away.

"By my boots and breeches!"

burst out a little sailor
with a lot of red whiskers.

"Mocha Dick laughed at Stormalong

and

spit

in

his

eye!"

All the sailors began to laugh
so hard that they almost went
to the bottom of the sea.
They laughed
until their sides ached,
and then they laughed some more.
They were still laughing
when the *Dolphin*
caught up with them.
"What's so funny?"
asked Captain Skinner
after the men
had climbed on board.

**"Mocha Dick laughed
at Stormalong
and spit in his eye!"**
said the little sailor
with red whiskers.

Captain Skinner began to laugh
so hard
that the first mate
had to grab him
by the seat of his pants
to keep him
from falling overboard.

"And Stormalong,
the man who boasted
that he would capture
Mocha Dick!" sputtered the captain.

"Ho, ho! Ha, ha!"

"Ho, ho! Ha, ha! Har, har!"

laughed the sailors.
"Ho, har!"
The little sailor with red whiskers
began to sing:

"Stormalong said he'd get Mocha Dick,
    Aye, mates, 'tis no lie,
But the Great White Whale
Just laughed in his face,
    And spit right in his eye.
To my aye, aye,
    right in Stormalong's eye,
To my aye, aye,
    Mister Stormalong's eye."

Stormalong felt so ashamed
that he went below and didn't
come up
on deck
for
a
week.

For three more months the *Dolphin* sailed the Pacific.
Stormalong did his share of the work,
but he never hooted like a foghorn
or whistled shrill like the wind in the rigging.
He hardly said a word.
When the *Dolphin* slid into the harbor at Nantucket,
the sailors told everyone what had happened.
Soon all Nantucket knew
that Mocha Dick had laughed at Stormalong and spit in his eye.
Poor Stormalong ran away to the beach where he could be alone.
All day long he sat on the beach, sighing and sighing.
He sighed so hard that the sea became choppy.
At last Stormalong picked himself up
and walked to the Sailors' Snug Haven.
The first thing he saw when he entered the inn
was the slate hanging over the fireplace.
  And on it were the words:

ON THIS VOYAGE OF THE
        DOLPHIN
  I WILL CAPTURE MOCHA
                        DICK
SIGNED ALFRED BULLTOP
                STORMALONG

Below these words someone had written:

BUT THE GREAT WHITE WHALE
    JUST
      LAUGHED AT HIM
        AND SPIT IN HIS EYE

Stormalong sat down
and ordered some shark soup,
which he drank from a dory.
He topped it off
with a keg of New England rum,
then went over to Captain Skinner
and said, "Captain,
I've made my last voyage."

"Surely not, laddie,"
said Captain Skinner kindly.
"Oh, no!"

"Aye, Captain," said Stormalong. "I'll never go to sea again.
I'm going to be a farmer."

"*A farmer!*" said Captain Skinner.
"You'll never be a farmer, my lad.
You've got salt water in your veins.
Wherever you go, you'll hear the sea calling to you."

"No," said Stormalong. "They don't build ships big enough for me.
I can't get the kinks out of my muscles.
And if I can't get the kinks out of my muscles,
I can't capture Mocha Dick.
And if I can't capture Mocha Dick, I'm no whaler.
And if I'm no whaler, I'm no sailor.
And if I'm no sailor, the sea is no place for me.

I'm going off to be a farmer."

"Well, lad," said Captain Skinner,
"if you must go, you must.
Good luck to you,
and may you reach a safe harbor.
But you'll be coming back to sea
someday.
And when you do,
old Captain Joshua Skinner
will give you a berth."

"Thank you, Captain,"
said Stormalong.
"Good-by, Captain."

The next morning
Stormalong left Nantucket
for the mainland.
His duffel bag over his shoulder,
he walked down the road.
In the light of the morning sun,
his shadow stretched before him
three counties long.
Stormalong rambled
about the Hudson Valley,
then stepped
over the Allegheny Mountains
and ambled
about the Shenandoah
Valley.

He took a little side trip
to the Cumberland Mountains
and spent a day
in the Tennessee Valley.
He walked along the Ohio River,
then over the rolling hills
of Indiana
and the prairies of Illinois.
But not until he crossed
the Mississippi River to Missouri
did he find
what he was looking for.

"Aye," said Stormalong,
"this is a country
where a full-sized man
can get the kinks
out of his muscles."

He was in a great forest,
where men with axes
were chopping down trees.
"Clong! Clong!" went the axes,
and the trees crashed
to the ground.

"Are you farmers, mateys?"
asked Stormalong
in his foghorn voice.
All the men stopped their work
to look at him.

"I reckon we are,"
said one of the men.

"That's good," said Stormalong
"I'm new to farming,
and I'll thank you to tell me
what to do."

"Right now
we're clearing away the forest
so's we can grow our crops,"
was the answer.

Stormalong borrowed
the biggest ax they had,
then said,
"Now, mates, just sit down
in the shade
and rest a while.
I mean to do
some plain and fancy chopping
to get the kinks
out of my muscles."

Stormalong rolled up his sleeves
and went to work.
By nightfall
he had cleared enough land
for a hundred farms.

"Who are you?"
asked the astonished farmers.

"Alfred Bulltop Stormalong
  is the name, mateys,"
  said Stormalong.
"They don't make ships
  big enough for me,
  so I can't get the kinks
  out of my muscles.
  If I can't get the kinks
  out of my muscles,
  I can't capture Mocha Dick.
  And
  if I can't capture Mocha Dick,
  I'm no whaler.
  And if I'm no whaler,
  then I'm no sailor.
  And if I'm no sailor,
  my place is on shore.
  So I came out here
  to be a farmer,
  and I'll thank you to tell me
  just what to do,
  and how to do it."

And he hooted like a foghorn
  and whistled shrill
  like the wind in the rigging.
"The next thing is to clear out
  the stumps and stones
  and start planting,"
  said the farmers.
"But first
  you'd better build yourself
  a cabin to live in."

"A cabin it is, me hearties,"
  said Stormalong.
  By the time the moon came out,
  he had built himself a cabin.

The next morning
  Stormalong got up
  before the sun
  and started to plow.
  He didn't use a horse.
  He just pushed the plow along
        himself,
  while stones and stumps flew
  in all directions.

"Where's your horse?"
  asked the farmers,
  more astonished than ever.
"We've never heard tell
  of plowing
without a horse or mule
  or at least a team of oxen."
They shook their heads.
"Didn't know
  you were supposed to have one,"
  said Stormalong.
"But no harm done.
  If you'll just toss these rocks
  and stumps into a pile,
I'll finish this little job."
By the time it was evening,
Stormalong had plowed
  enough land
  for a hundred farms.

"What's next, me hearties?"
  he asked.
"For I've got the kinks
  out of my muscles,
  and I'm rarin' to go."

"Plant the seed,"
  said the farmers.

When the farmers got up
  the next morning,
  they found Stormalong
  stretched out under a tree.

"Glad you're up," he said.
"I've planted all the seed.
  Nothing to it.
  What do I do now?"
"Just wait for the crops
  to start growing,"
  said the farmers.
"Unless you have some cows
  or chickens or pigs
  to look after."

"I can't look after cows
  or chickens or pigs,"
  said Stormalong.
"I'm too big for 'em.
  But I don't like this idea
  of waiting.
  I'll get kinks in my muscles."

It was hard for Stormalong
to sit around doing nothing.
At night he could hear the wind blowing
through the trees of the forest.
The leaves went hiss, swish,
like the sound of the sea.
The branches creaked
like the rigging of a ship.
Stormalong dreamed
that he was a sailor again.

In the daytime
Stormalong would climb
the tallest tree in the forest.
He would gaze out over the rolling hills,
which looked like the waves of the sea.
The tree swayed in the wind,
and Stormalong imagined
he was in the crow's nest of the *Dolphin*,
keeping a sharp lookout for whale.

A big cloud floated past in the sky.
To Stormalong
it looked like Mocha Dick.

"Blo-o-ows!" he shouted.
"Thar she blows!
Whale off the starboard side!
Thar she blows and breaches!
And Mocha Dick, at that!
After him, me hearties!
A dead whale or a stove boat!"

Then one day a storm came up.
The sky was as black as the bottom of a well.
Lightning flashed, thunder roared,
while the wind went howling through the forest like a madman.

"Hooray, a storm!" shouted Stormalong to the farmers.
"Now I can get the kinks out of my muscles.
  Avast there, mateys! Storm ahead! All hands on deck!"

All of a sudden one of the farmers
stuck his head out of the window of his cabin,
and looked at Stormalong.
"What's all the fuss?" he asked.

"Storm!" said Stormalong. "Pipe all hands on deck!
What do farmers do in a storm, matey?"

"Let 'er storm," said the farmer. "Nothing else to do."

Stormalong was so surprised he couldn't say anything.
He just stood there, the lightning flashing around his head,
the rain dripping down his shoulders.

"I've had enough of this," he said at last.
"I can't sit around and do nothing when there's a storm.
I guess I just wasn't cut out to be a farmer."

He went to his cabin, threw his duffel bag over his shoulder,
then waved good-by to the farmers.

"So long," he said. "I'm going west to be a cowboy."

Stormalong rambled about the dusty plains of Texas,
then ambled over to Oklahoma.
He took a side trip to the Rocky Mountains
and followed the Sweetwater River into Wyoming.
He walked across the salt flats of Utah and the plateau of Arizona,
but not until he came to New Mexico
did he find what he was looking for.

"Aye," he said, "this is a country
where a full-sized man can get the kinks out of his muscles."

Stormalong went into a store to buy himself a cowboy outfit.
"Matey," he said to the storekeeper, "I want a ten-gallon hat,
chaps, a checkered shirt, Spanish boots with pointed toes,
silver spurs, and a pretty bandana."

The storekeeper looked Stormalong up and down.
"Stranger," he said, "you're the biggest galoot
that ever blew into this man's town.
I can sell you what you want,
but it will have to be made special."
It took eight weeks to make
Stormalong's cowboy outfit.
While he was waiting,
Stormalong learned how to use a lariat.
With his lariat he lassoed a wild mustang
that roamed the plains.

The
mustang was
a little too small
for Stormalong,
but it was the biggest horse
he could get.

Then Stormalong got a job
as a cowboy
on the Triple Star Ranch.

"Mateys," he said,
"I've never been a cowboy before,
and I'll thank you to tell me what to do."

"It's round-up time, pardner," said the cowboys.
"First thing to do is round up the steers."

"Just sit down and rest yourselves, me hearties,"
said Stormalong.
"I'll round 'em up,
just to get the kinks out of my muscles."

When evening came, Stormalong had
rounded up all the steers.

"Who are you?" asked the astonished cowboys.

"Alfred Bulltop Stormalong is the name,"
answered Stormalong.
"They don't make ships big enough for me,
so I can't get the kinks out of my muscles.
If I can't get the kinks out of my muscles,
I can't capture Mocha Dick.
And if I can't capture Mocha Dick, I'm no whaler.
And if I'm no whaler, then I'm no sailor.
And if I'm no sailor, my place is on shore.
I tried to be a farmer, but I couldn't.
So I came out here to be a cowboy,
and I'll thank you to tell me what to do."

"The next thing to do is brand the steers," said the cowboys.

Stormalong got up before the sun the next morning
and started to brand the steers.
By the time the cowboys got up, all the steers had been branded.
"What's next, me hearties?" asked Stormalong.
"For I've got the kinks out of my muscles, and I'm rarin' to go."

"Just ride around and keep an eye on the steers.
We call it riding herd," said the cowboys.

Stormalong rode herd with the other cowboys.
At night they sat around the campfire, playing the guitar
and singing songs. Stormalong had a guitar made special,
and when he played it, the mountains would echo for miles around.
Stormalong soon began to get tired of being a cowboy.
There wasn't enough to do, and he was getting kinks in his muscles.
At night he would wake up and look around. In the moonlight
the plain stretched out like a calm sea, while the mountains stood up
like islands.

"Avast, mateys!" shouted Stormalong. "We're becalmed!
More sail, more sail! Break out more sail, me hearties,
for we must capture Mocha Dick, the Great White Whale!"

One day a huge black cloud filled the sky, and the rain began to come down.
Lightning flashed, thunder boomed, and the wind raced
across the plain like wild horses.

Stormalong waved his ten-gallon hat in the air and shouted,
"All hands on deck!
Storm blowing up!
All hands on deck!"
And he hooted like a foghorn and whistled shrill
like the wind in the rigging.

"What's the rumpus, pardner?" asked one of the cowboys.

"Storm!" said Stormalong. "What do cowboys do in a storm, matey?
She's a-rippin' and a-snortin'."

"Let 'er rip and snort," said the cowboy. "Nothing else to do about it."

Stormalong sat down on a big rock. The wind howled around him,
and the water dripped off his hat like a waterfall.

"I just can't sit around and do nothing
  when there's a storm," he said.
"I guess I'm no more a cowboy than I was a farmer."

Stormalong seemed to hear the voice of Captain Skinner saying,
"Aye, lad, you'll never be able to give up the sea.
  You've got salt water in your veins.
  Wherever you go, you'll hear the sea calling to you."

"You were right, Captain Skinner!" shouted Stormalong.
"Maybe the ships are too small for a full-sized man.
  Maybe I'll get kinks in my muscles
  and won't be able to capture Mocha Dick.
  Maybe I'm no whaler, and maybe I'm no sailor.
  But I'll go back to sea if I have to be a cabin boy,
  for I'll never be happy anywhere else."

Stormalong turned his mustang loose on the plains.
He threw his duffel bag over one shoulder
  and slung his guitar over the other.

"So long, mateys," he said to the cowboys.
  Then he started walking east, toward Nantucket and the sea.

It was a wet, misty morning when Stormalong got to Nantucket. For a long time he stood on a hill, sniffing in the salt sea air. He could see the harbor with masts of ships sticking up into the sky. When he caught sight of the waves breaking on the shore, he hooted like a foghorn and whistled shrill like the wind in the rigging.

"The sea is the place for me," he said.
"And now for the Sailors' Snug Haven
and some of that good shark soup."

When Stormalong got to the Sailors' Snug Haven,
he wiped the mist from his eyes and looked around.
Everything was the same as it had been.
Over the fireplace hung the slate with these words on it:

ON THIS VOYAGE OF THE
DOLPHIN
i WILL CAPTURE MOCHA
DiCK
SiGNED ALFRED BULLTOP
STORMALONG

BUT THE GREAT WHITE WHALE
JUST
LAUGHED AT HiM
AND SPiT iN HiS EYE

"A cowboy in Nantucket!" said a voice behind him.
"You're a long way from home, matey."

Stormalong turned around. There sat Captain Skinner.

"The sea is my home, Captain," said Stormalong,
hooting like a foghorn and whistling shrill like the wind in the rigging.

"By my boots and breeches!" said the captain.
"It's Stormalong, for there's no one else who can hoot like a foghorn
and whistle shrill like the wind in the rigging."

"Aye," said Stormalong, "Alfred Bulltop Stormalong it is,
and I'll never leave the sea again."

"I knew you'd be back, lad," said Captain Skinner.
"Now sit down beside me and tell me your adventures."

Stormalong ordered some shark soup,
which he drank from a dory.
He told Captain Skinner all his adventures,
and when he had finished, he said:

"And now, Captain,
will you give me my old berth
on the *Dolphin?*"

"Aye, laddie.
But you used to complain
that the *Dolphin*
was too small for you.
Well, she's still the same size,
but you're bigger than ever."

"She'll be big enough for me,"
said Stormalong.
"I'll go to sea in a washtub
if I can't get anything else."

353

"Spoken like a true seaman!"
laughed Captain Skinner.
"Well, I must leave you now,
for I've some business to do.
We sail at six
tomorrow morning.
Be sure that you're on time."

When Captain Skinner stood up,
Stormalong saw
that one of his legs was gone.
In its place was a wooden peg leg.

"Your leg, Captain!" said Stormalong.
"What happened?"

"It was bit off by Mocha Dick on my last voyage.
  The white whale bit off my leg
  and sent two of my crew to the bottom of the sea."

"Captain Skinner," cried Stormalong,
  "I won't rest until I've captured Mocha Dick."

"No, lad," said the captain.
"Never again will I battle Mocha Dick.
  He's more fearful than ever.
  I'll lose no more of my men to the monster."
And with that he left the inn.

When Stormalong came on board the *Dolphin* the next morning,
  the crew began to laugh.
  He was still wearing his cowboy outfit,
  and he was so bowlegged from riding the mustang
  that a ship could have sailed between his legs.

"Avast there, Stormalong!" said Captain Skinner.
"Get below and put on some proper duds.
  Stormalong or no Stormalong, I'll have no cowboys on my ship."

"Captain, I'd like to do as you say,
  but this cowboy outfit was made special,
  and I'm going to keep on wearing it."

Captain Skinner grew red in the face.

"I'm captain of this ship, and you'll obey my orders!" he roared.

"Captain," said Stormalong, "I know you're the captain.
But captain or no captain, I'm going to wear my cowboy outfit."

Stormalong began to hop up and down,
so that the *Dolphin* rocked in the water.

"Belay there, Stormalong!" shouted the sailors.
"Sit down, you're rocking the boat!"

"Stop, Stormalong! You'll sink the ship!" cried the captain.

Stormalong kept hopping up and down.

"I won't stop until you say it's all right
for me to wear my cowboy outfit," he said.
"And you can lay to that!"

"Wear what you like, you stubborn walrus!" said the captain,
and Stormalong stopped hopping up and down.

A crowd had gathered on shore
to say good-by to Captain Skinner and his crew.

"Good luck!" they called. "A short voyage and a greasy one!"

Captain Skinner was so angry that he didn't want to say good-by
to anyone.

"CAST OFF!" he bellowed.

The *Dolphin* was raring to go.
She took the wind in her sails and made for the open sea.

It was not long before the lookout in the crow's nest sang out,
"Blo-o-ows! Thar she blows! Whale off the port side!"

shouted Stormalong, like a cowboy.
Still dressed in his cowboy outfit,
he jumped into his boat.
It made Captain Skinner angry
to see a cowboy in a whaling boat.
But he didn't say anything. He was afraid
Stormalong would start hopping up and down again.

Stormalong soon showed that he could still catch whales.

"By the Great Horn Spoon," said Captain Skinner to himself,
"Stormalong is a real sailorman,
even if he does dress like a cowboy."

Then one day
the lookout in the crow's nest shouted,
"Blo-o-ows! Thar she blows and breaches!
And Mocha Dick, at that!
It's the Great White Whale, mates!"

"All hands aloft!" ordered Captain Skinner.
"Break out more sail.
We're going to get away from these waters as fast as we can.
I'll not battle Mocha Dick again."

"Captain," said Stormalong,
"are you really going to let it be said
that a Nantucket whaler ran away from a whale?"

"Mocha Dick is no ordinary whale. He is a monster,
and I'll lose no more of my men to him," said Captain Skinner.

"Let me go after him," begged Stormalong.
"He'll not laugh at me this time."

"Stow your chatter and help loose the sails,"
Captain Skinner bellowed.
"I'm the captain of the *Dolphin*, Mr. Stormalong,
and I forbid you to go after Mocha Dick.

Now get aloft before I have you put in irons!"

But just then
the lookout in the crow's nest
gave a terrible cry.

"Mocha Dick is coming after us!
He's going to bump the ship!"

Captain Skinner ran to the rail.
There was Mocha Dick roaring and snorting and plunging.
He rushed straight at the *Dolphin*, and "**Bump!**"
The stern of the ship rose into the air.

"We are lost!" cried the sailors.
"Mocha Dick will sink the ship. We are lost!"

"Not yet, mateys!"
said Stormalong.

And leaping over the rail,
he landed smack
on Mocha Dick's back.

"Yippee!" shouted Stormalong,
and he began to ride Mocha Dick
like a cowboy riding a bucking bronco.
He hung on with one hand
and waved his ten-gallon hat with the other.

Mocha Dick thrashed about,
trying to throw Stormalong
off his back.

Stormalong only laughed
and waved his hat again.

"Ride him, cowboy!"
cheered the sailors.
"Ride him, Stormalong!"

Snorting with rage,
the white whale leaped
into the air.
Then he dove deep
under the water,
trying to drown
Stormalong.
But Stormalong
took a deep breath
and held his nose.

Mocha Dick heaved himself into the air again.
He tossed and twisted
and turned.

Then
he began
to swim
furiously
about.
He went zig-zag

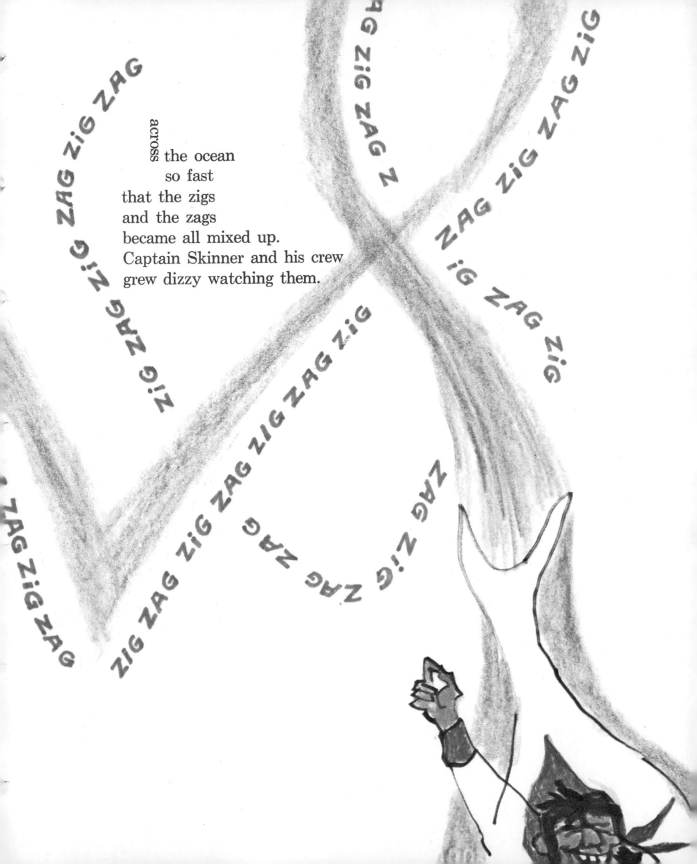

across the ocean
   so fast
that the zigs
and the zags
became all mixed up.
Captain Skinner and his crew
grew dizzy watching them.

"Ride him, cowboy!" they yelled. "Ride him, Stormalong!"

"Yippee! Wahoo!" shouted Stormalong,
hooting like a foghorn
and whistling shrill like the wind in the rigging.

For three days Stormalong rode Mocha Dick.
Once when he passed close to the ship, he called out,
"I'm getting hungry, mates.
How about some coffee and a sandwich?"

The cook made him a washtub of coffee
and a sandwich three yards long.
When Stormalong passed by again,
a sailor stood on the jib boom
and handed them to Stormalong.

On the third day
Mocha Dick's strength was almost gone.

But he made one great try
to throw Stormalong off his back.
He dove deep under the water.
He turned somersaults.
He tossed and twisted and rolled from side to side.
He went around in circles, like a dog chasing his tail.
Around and around he went,
until the water foamed like milk.
He leaped high into the air and came down
with a tremendous splash.
Then a shudder ran through his body,
and he was still.

"Hooray!" shouted the sailors.
"Hooray for Stormalong!"

"This is the end of the Great White Whale,"
 said a big sailor with a crooked nose.
"He just wore himself out."

"No," said a little sailor with red whiskers,
"he died of a broken heart."

"Hooray!" shouted the sailors again and again.
"Hooray for Stormalong!"

"Aye, lads, you may well cheer,"
 said Captain Skinner.
"Stormalong has done a great thing.
 No more will Mocha Dick
 send honest seamen to their death."

Then the *Dolphin* dropped anchor
beside the huge body of the white whale.
The sailors cut him up
and boiled the blubber for the sperm oil.

In a few days the job was done,
and they set sail for Nantucket.

"We're loaded to the hatches with oil.
We'll all be rich," said Captain Skinner.
He felt so happy
that he danced a hornpipe across the deck.
Tappy, tappy, tap went his peg leg.

Stormalong sat down on a hatch
and rested his feet on the jib boom.
He picked up his guitar and began
to sing loud and gay.

"Twang, twang! Plunk, plunk! Plunkety, twang!" went the guitar.
The deep notes sounded like a pipe organ, and the high notes
were as sweet as violins. Stormalong sang "Home on the Range"
and "Bury Me Not on the Lone Prairie."

The crew came back with "Blow the Man Down."
Stormalong topped them with
"As I Was Walking Down the Streets of Laredo."
Then they all chimed in
with "Whiskey for My Johnnie."

The sound of their music
was so sweet
that all the fish
lifted their heads
out of the water
to listen.

Sea gulls flew after the ship,
beating their wings in time to the music.
All the way across the ocean
the fish followed the *Dolphin*.
In schools and shoals and droves they came,
and the New England fishermen
caught the greatest catch of seafish
that was ever caught in all history.

When the *Dolphin* got into Nantucket,
the crew was singing, each man-jack louder than the next:

"Then give me a whaleman, wherever he be,
Who fears not a fish that can swim the salt sea;
Then give me a tight ship, and under snug sail,
And last lay me 'side the noble sperm whale;
In the Indian Ocean,
Or Pacific Ocean,
No matter *what* ocean;
Pull ahead, yo heave O!"

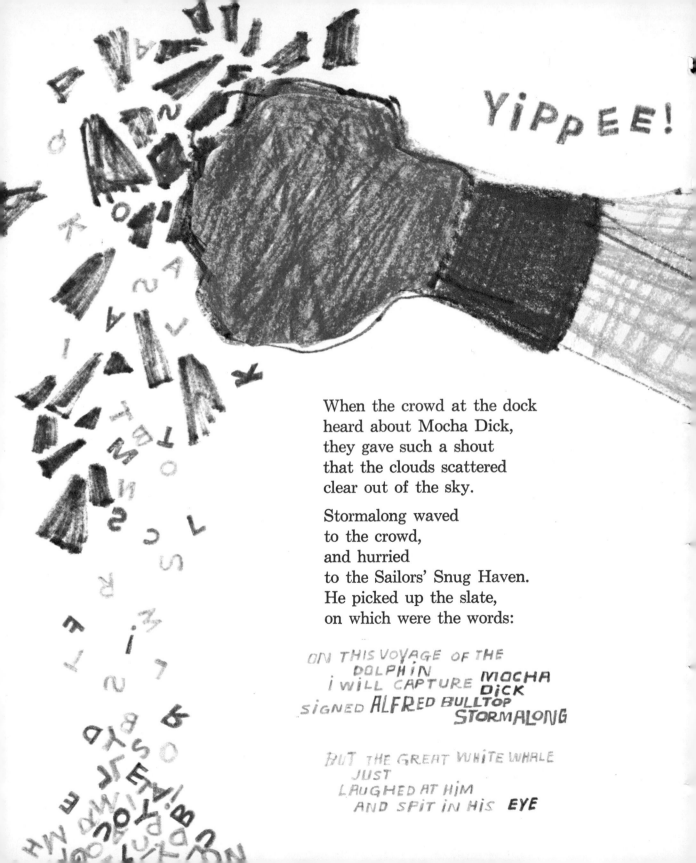

YIPPEE!

When the crowd at the dock
heard about Mocha Dick,
they gave such a shout
that the clouds scattered
clear out of the sky.

Stormalong waved
to the crowd,
and hurried
to the Sailors' Snug Haven.
He picked up the slate,
on which were the words:

ON THIS VOYAGE OF THE
DOLPHIN
I WILL CAPTURE MOCHA
DICK
SIGNED ALFRED BULLTOP
STORMALONG

BUT THE GREAT WHITE WHALE
JUST
LAUGHED AT HIM
AND SPIT IN HIS EYE

"No more he doesn't!" shouted Stormalong.

He smashed the slate into a thousand pieces.

"Mateys," he roared, "I captured Mocha Dick.
If I captured Mocha Dick, I'm a whaler.
And if I'm a whaler, then I'm a sailor.
And if I'm a sailor, my place is on the sea.
And the sea is no place for a cowboy.
I'll never wear my cowboy outfit again,
even though it was made special.
And you can lay to that!"

Then Stormalong sat down and ate twelve dozen oysters,
fifty-two codfish balls, sixty-seven lobsters,
ten pounds of whale steak,
a dory full of shark soup,
and another full of clam chowder.
For dessert he had a New England boiled dinner,
three or four apple pies,
and a nibble or two of maple sugar candy.
He washed it all down
with a keg of New England rum,
then hooted like a foghorn
and whistled shrill
like the wind in the rigging.

"Hooray for Old Stormalong!"
shouted all the crew.

"Hooray, hooray,
hooray!"

After staying on shore for a week,
Stormalong sailed off again on the *Dolphin*.
He made many voyages in many ships,
until Donald McKay built a ship called the *Courser*.
She was so big the captain and his officers
had to ride around on horseback.
The mast was so tall
that it had to be bent back on hinges
to let the sun and moon go past.

When Stormalong saw the *Courser*, he said,
"There's my ship," and asked the captain for a berth.

BUT THAT'S ANOTHER STORY.

Wild Bugles of the Mountains

SNOWBOUND

The Coin

Spring

Guatemalan Market

The Princess and the Vagabone

swoosh!

The Two Frogs

SPEECH IS THE NET IN WHICH OUR ARE DREAMS CAUGHT

Old Stormalong

A Birthday

Goody O'Grumpity

MEAT, MATÉ and MUSIC

The Top Speeds of Animals

Piasa

Tree

FOOD

The Pioneer

The Selfish Giant

making judgments

Have you read the Table of Contents
in *Sounds of a Distant Drum* lately?
Or have you browsed through the book,
remembering your reactions to the various selections?
Now might be a good time
to organize your judgments about this book.
You can do this by reading the titles
and looking once again at the pages,
deciding as you go along which are your favorites.

Is it difficult or easy for you to determine
your five favorite stories? your five favorite poems?
your five favorite articles? your five favorite pictures?
Do you have any notion why you make the choices you do?
Restricting your various kinds of choices
to five selections in each category
will help to shed light on your system of choosing,
especially if you have several selections
that you find difficult to eliminate.

PROUD PEACOCK
using your ears in reading
up over the trees. It went on and on. It was just a speck in the distance
SPACE SHIP BIFROST
What Is Black?
The Stone
OUR COUNTRY
The Cataract of Lodore
PEAS
The Quail
Time Line into Space
BRIGHTY
plugging into meanings
A DAY AT HOME in Uganda
A Turkey Speaks: The Ride-By-Nights Up on their brooms the Witches stream

Illustration by Frank Aloise

And what about the items you reject?
"What is there about any one selection
that makes me prefer it over the others?"
you will keep asking yourself.
And gradually you will come to know your various standards
for making judgments about literature and art and language.

I am sure that you have noticed
the many styles of writing and many kinds of illustrating
used in *Sounds of a Distant Drum.*
This was done deliberately.
As you encounter the many different ways
that words and color
and shape and texture can be used to express an idea,
you will begin to know which are most appealing to you.

It has been said that we live in a world of choice.
This is indeed true
when you are involved
in reading and viewing the printed page.
So, on with your choosing.
Which are your five favorites?

An essay by Bill Martin, Jr.

383

The Sun

This burst
Of joy;
This thrust
From space
Into the eye
And heart.

This part
Of life
So far away
That sweat
And tears
Are never far apart.

This healing glow;
This gift
To poor
And sick—
This quick
Star-spanning
Light
That rides
The day
And ends the night.

A poem by Michael Geelan,
painting by William Andrews